THE GLOBAL GAG RULE AND WOMEN'S
REPRODUCTIVE HEALTH

THE GLOBAL GAG
RULE AND WOMEN'S
REPRODUCTIVE HEALTH

Rhetoric Versus Reality

Yana van der Meulen Rodgers

OXFORD
UNIVERSITY PRESS

OXFORD
UNIVERSITY PRESS

Oxford University Press is a department of the University of Oxford. It furthers
the University's objective of excellence in research, scholarship, and education
by publishing worldwide. Oxford is a registered trade mark of Oxford University
Press in the UK and certain other countries.

Published in the United States of America by Oxford University Press
198 Madison Avenue, New York, NY 10016, United States of America.

Library of Congress Cataloging-in-Publication Data
Names: Rodgers, Yana van der Meulen, author.
Title: The global gag rule and women's reproductive health : rhetoric versus reality /
Yana van der Meulen Rodgers.
Description: New York : Oxford University Press, [2018] |
Includes bibliographical references and index.
Identifiers: LCCN 2018012987 (print) | LCCN 2018026194 (ebook) |
ISBN 9780190876135 (UPDF) | ISBN 9780190876142 (EPUB) |
ISBN 9780190876128 (hardcover : alk. paper)
Subjects: LCSH: Abortion—Government policy—United States. | Abortion—Law and
legislation—United States. | Reproductive rights—United States. |
Family planning—United States. | Abortion—Government policy—Developing countries. |
Abortion—Law and legislation—Developing countries. |
Reproductive rights—Developing countries. | Family planning—Developing countries.
Classification: LCC HQ767.5.U5 (ebook) | LCC HQ767.5.U5 R627 2018 (print) |
DDC 362.1988/800973—dc23
LC record available at https://lccn.loc.gov/2018012987

1 3 5 7 9 8 6 4 2

Printed by Sheridan Books, Inc., United States of America

CONTENTS

ACKNOWLEDGMENTS

A number of people have provided invaluable comments and suggestions on this project at various stages of the research and writing. Lee Badgett, Giselle Carino, Don Carroll, Bergen Cooper, Barbara Crane, Nancy Folbre, Sarah Gammage, Mary Hawkesworth, Joel Heisey, Dorothy Hodgson, Marlene Lee, Carl Lin, Jasbir Puar, Shahra Razavi, Vanessa Rios, Charles Schlenker, Barbara Seligman, Diana Strassmann, Siri Suh, and Myra Strober each played an important role in helping the research and the book to take shape. A special acknowledgment goes to Cathy Blackwell, Danny Blitzer, Diane Fay, Victoria Floor, Mary Fowler, Jay Friedman, Debra Grady, Jessica Mazzeo, Billy Rodgers, Charlie Rodgers, and Cathy Wheeler for their help with proofreading and editing, and to Cynthia Daniels for her comprehensive comments on my proposal and research agenda.

I also gratefully acknowledge my home institution, Rutgers University, for granting me a research sabbatical that allowed the much-needed time to work on this project, and for approving my Institutional Review Board application to conduct interviews (IRB Protocol # E18-028). Workshop participants at the Center for Health and Gender Equity, International Center for Research on Women, International Women's Health Coalition, UN Women, International Planned Parenthood Federation / Western Hemisphere Region, and the University of Wisconsin–Whitewater provided useful comments. Many thanks also to Kanani Kauka at the Kaiser Family Foundation for providing additional descriptive statistics. I am indebted to Eran Bendavid and Grant Miller for sharing with me their detailed methodological appendix and Stata files, which proved instrumental in completing the empirical work. David Pervin provided outstanding guidance and editorial expertise every step of the way. I am especially grateful to Jay Friedman for his incredible support and care during the writing process.

THE GLOBAL GAG RULE AND WOMEN'S REPRODUCTIVE HEALTH

Chapter 1

Introduction

In recent decades, the long arm of US politics has reached the intimate lives and reproductive health of women all over the world. Since 1984, healthcare organizations in developing countries that provide family-planning services have faced several waves of cuts in US foreign aid. These restrictions originated in a 1984 ruling known as the Mexico City Policy (named after the location of a conference where the policy was first announced) in which the US government would cut off family-planning assistance to any nongovernmental organization (NGO) that performs or promotes abortions as a method of family planning. The ruling, commonly referred to as the global gag rule, prohibits even counseling women on abortion or advocating for the legalization of abortion, thus effectively placing a gag on healthcare providers' freedom of speech. It applies only to nongovernmental organizations overseas; foreign governments, multilateral agencies, and US nonprofit organizations are exempt. Most US financial assistance for family planning takes the form of bilateral aid (aid from one country to another) as opposed to funds channeled through multilateral organizations. Thus, with its restrictions on bilateral aid for family planning, the global gag rule is a good example of how the US government can use foreign aid to achieve political objectives.

Since its adoption by President Ronald Reagan in 1984, the policy has remained a hallmark of Republican administrations, with alternating revocations and restorations of the policy by successive US presidents depending on their party affiliation. The global gag rule was rescinded by Bill Clinton in 1993, reinstated by George W. Bush in 2001, rescinded by Barack Obama in 2009, and reinstated again in 2017 under Donald

Trump. This policy came on top of legislation in place since 1973 (the Helms Amendment) prohibiting the use of US foreign assistance to pay for abortions as a method of family planning. Under the global gag rule, foreign NGOs cannot even use their own funding for abortion-related activities; they must agree to comply with the policy or their US assistance for family planning is terminated. Not only was the global gag rule reinstated in 2017, it was also dramatically expanded upon previous iterations of the policy. Specifically, the expanded version ends family-planning assistance (which amounts to about $600 million per year) to NGOs that provide abortion services, counsel patients about abortion options, or advocate for the liberalization of abortion laws. It also extends the target of the cuts to all global health funding (a substantially larger pot of about $10 billion per year).

The 2017 reinstatement of the policy has prompted a new round of heated debate in media discourse on the motivation and repercussions of the restrictions on US financial assistance. The commentary has extended across all kinds of media sources and across the political divide, and projected impacts have varied widely. Proponents of the Mexico City Policy point to the importance of reducing the number of abortions globally and preventing foreign organizations from receiving US financial assistance if they perform abortions. For example, the National Right to Life Committee championed the reinstatement of the policy for "putting an end to taxpayer funding of groups that promote the killing of unborn children in developing nations" (NRLC, 2017). Arina Grossu from the Family Research Council issued a similar statement: "These radical abortion groups have been weaned off of American taxpayer dime and it should stay that way. American taxpayers should not be forced to partner with foreign organizations that kill babies internationally" (Grossu, 2017). The United States Conference of Catholic Bishops also applauded the 2017 reinstatement of the Mexico City Policy and claimed that "an overwhelming majority" of Americans support the policy (USCCB, 2017).

Critics argue that the global gag rule leads to more rather than fewer abortions because the restrictions on US family-planning assistance cause healthcare staff reductions, clinic closures, and contraceptive shortages. The decreased access to contraception and reproductive health services then contributes to more unintended pregnancies and more abortions.

They also argue that in the numerous countries where national legislation prohibits abortions in all cases or only to save the mother's life, most of the additional abortions are unsafe. For example, the Center for American Progress cautioned that the 2017 reinstatement of the global gag rule could cause more than 8 million women to suffer serious complications from unsafe abortions and another 289,000 women to die from pregnancy or childbirth related reasons (Center for American Progress, 2017). The president and CEO of the Guttmacher Institute predicted that millions of men, women, and children will experience negative consequences as a result of the extended global gag rule and the cuts in funding to vital health programs (Starrs, 2017). And in another example, a piece in *Foreign Policy* called the global gag rule "America's deadly export" and relayed widespread concerns that the US policy would reverse the small but essential gains that some of the poorest countries have made on safe abortion as well as the progress in increasing contraceptive access, reducing maternal mortality, and promoting women's rights (Filopovic, 2017).

The media exposure and coverage of the global gag rule is much heavier now than it was during previous administrations, not only because of the ubiquity of the internet and social media, but also because the global gag rule has become closely linked to Donald Trump's so-called war on women. It may be hard for skeptical observers to determine the extent to which the bold statements on both sides of the spectrum are closer to rhetoric or reality, particularly because there is very little statistical evidence on the actual impact of the global gag rule on women's reproductive health outcomes. To date, just two previous studies have quantified the impact of the global gag rule under George W. Bush beginning in 2001. Both of these studies focused on sub-Saharan Africa and both used econometric methods to show that the policy resulted in higher abortion rates in countries that depended on US financial assistance for family planning (Bendavid, Avila, and Miller, 2011; Jones, 2015). Additional qualitative evidence from a set of case study interviews conducted by a consortium of NGOs indicates that the 2001 reinstatement of the global gag rule caused substantial disruptions to the provision of family-planning services through clinic closures, staff reductions, and contraceptive shortages (PAI, 2005). Although the interviews did not generate estimates for the impact of the policy on women's reproductive health, it is likely that the disruptions to the provision of contraceptive methods increased the number of unintended pregnancies. More unintended pregnancies, in turn, would have resulted in higher fertility rates or more abortions or both.

One of the researchers who helped to conduct the Population Action International case studies reflected in a recent interview on the need for evidence on the impact of the global gag rule, which after the 2001 reinstatement by George W. Bush was virtually nonexistent. She said in the interview:

> There were people at the time who said, "Don't bother doing this because there's no way to get rid of the policy until the politics change," which in a way was true. But even then you need to have some evidence and data to strengthen the case and to make sure that even your allies are going to support you on an issue. I still think gathering the data and the evidence is really important even though the gag rule is very much a creature of the political to and fro that we have.[1]

Despite the importance of evidence on the global gag rule, there are very few other assessments of the actual impact of the policy on the provision of family-planning services and on women's reproductive health. This limited amount of evidence makes it difficult to ascertain the plausibility of the most recent claims in the media following Trump's reinstatement of the policy. Furthermore, numerous NGOs have issued reports about the scope of the global gag rule, and academic articles and book chapters have discussed the political context and history of the policy, but no books have woven together these accounts with original statistical evidence to provide a comprehensive study of the global gag rule. Similarly, although there is a voluminous literature on abortion within and outside of the United States, there is surprisingly little information about the empirical aspects of abortion, especially what kind of policy is most effective in reducing abortion rates (Kulczycki, 1999). The weight of the evidence points to greater access to modern contraception as one of the key means to reduce abortion, but the exact relationship between access to contraception and the incidence of abortion is still unknown, as are the other variables that determine women's decisions to have an abortion. National laws on abortion appear to play less of a role in influencing women's decisions regarding abortion.

This book aims to fill these gaps by conducting a systematic analysis of how the global gag rule affects women's reproductive health across all major developing regions of the world. More specifically, the book extends the focus of the two previous econometric studies of the impact of the 2001 global gag rule on abortion in sub-Saharan Africa to include three additional developing regions: Latin America and the Caribbean, Eastern Europe and Central Asia, and South and Southeast Asia. This statistical analysis is grounded in a conceptual framework that models the complex factors that influence women's decision-making about fertility. The book also examines restrictions on women's reproductive health more generally by using historical analysis, case studies, and analysis of aggregate data to examine the evolution of family-planning programs, the links between contraceptive access and fertility rates, and the relationship between restrictive national abortion laws and actual abortion rates. This mixed-methods approach sheds new light on the risks that women in different regions of the world face as a result of the global gag rule. The book also evaluates the likelihood of other policy impacts, including adverse effects for children's health and cuts in funding for HIV/AIDS prevention and treatment.

Although this study relies heavily on statistical methods, there are very real people and stories behind the numbers. Millions of women across developing regions have had their access to reproductive health services tied to swings in US presidential politics, and many of those women have experienced hardships as a result of clinic closures or reductions in services and supplies. Their stories illustrate how extremes in American politics can influence the private lives of women throughout the developing world. One of many such examples comes from an NGO called Family Health Options Kenya, which lost $620,000 in USAID funding in 2017 after it refused to comply with the terms of the global gag rule. This loss, which amounted to almost 20% of the NGO's budget, forced the organization in 2017 to close one clinic, lay off 20 employees including nurses and pharmacists, terminate many of its free outreach visits to rural communities, and start charging for services that used to be free (PBS, 2017; Swetlitz, 2017). Two of the organization's directors, Melvine Ouyo and Amos Simpano, have been proactive in telling their story to the media. Ouyo said that in October 2017, a 15-year-old pregnant girl hanged herself because she did not have access to any medical care; this girl lived in a community that Family Health Options Kenya could not reach due to lack of funding. Simpano also expressed concerns about needing to terminate a long-term intervention in which his medical staff worked with religious leaders to teach young women about birth control in predominantly Muslim communities where many believed that the Koran forbade modern contraceptives. Simpano said in an interview, "I think the communities will feel that we have betrayed them," and he worried that women would return to feeling constrained in choosing modern contraception because of their religion (Swetlitz, 2017). One of the NGO's patients, Elizabeth Wanjiru, could afford to start paying for contraceptive services that used to be free, but she said that many of her friends could not: "They're not using family planning. And if they're not using family planning, they end up having baby, unwanted pregnancy" (PBS, 2017).

Another story illustrates how the impacts of US funding restrictions go beyond women's reproductive health. Not only have Republican administrations implemented the restrictions through the global gag rule, since 1986 they have also been defunding the United Nations Population Fund (UNFPA), the United Nations agency that promotes family planning and women's reproductive rights. Mirroring the pattern of the global gag rule, Democratic administrations have subsequently restored the funding after each cycle of defunding. In a story told by Dr. Natalia Kanem, the executive director of UNFPA as of October 2017, she describes a visit to a mobile maternal health clinic in the conflict-ridden city of Homs, Syria, earlier in the year. A woman anxiously approached Dr. Kanem at the clinic, not because of pregnancy, but for assistance in getting her husband's blood pressure medication. Trump's announcement in January 2017 that the United States would withhold financial support from the UNFPA left a $70 million gap in the agency's budget, placing UNFPA-funded health facilities such as the mobile clinic in Homs, Syria, at serious risk of staffing shortages, medication shortfalls, and even closure (Gladstone, 2017). As the story demonstrates, it is not just contraceptive access that is disrupted by the US funding restrictions but also life-saving drugs for community members served by the clinics.

In the Democratic Republic of Congo, one of the largest reproductive health organizations—ABEF, or the Association pour le Bien-Etre Familial/Naissances Désirables—does not provide abortion services, so it is technically complying with the terms of the global gag rule. Even so, as of November 2017 ABEF expected to lose about 70% of its budget because two of its largest funders, the International Planned Parenthood Federation and the UNFPA, have both had their funding cut by the US government (Kasinof, 2017). The International Planned Parenthood Federation expects to lose about $100 million in funding as a result of its decision not to comply with the global gag rule, and the UNFPA was defunded by the Trump administration. Jeannine Assani, regional coordinator for ABEF in the Congo, worried that the restrictions would seriously compromise the ability of ABEF to continue its provision of free contraceptives, gynecological exams, and family-planning counseling. In an interview with Public Radio International, she stated, "Now we can't even really supply condoms. . . . Women will come here, but often we have to refer them to the main hospital where they have to pay" (Kasinof, 2017).

These stories provide additional motivation for producing new statistical evidence on the impact of the global gag rule because often legislative changes are prompted not only by gripping narratives and compelling qualitative evidence but also by rigorous quantitative analysis. Collectively, the remaining chapters build the foundations upon which the empirical analysis of foreign aid and reproductive health is based. To commence the study, Chapter 2 offers a detailed account of the evolution of the global gag rule and the existing evidence on its effects. When it was announced in Mexico City, the policy created an international firestorm with its abrupt change in position on population control and abortion as a method of family planning. Pressure from domestic antiabortion groups weighed heavily in the administration's new policy stance on family-planning assistance. Subsequent rescissions and reinstatements of the global gag rule have led to noticeable fluctuations in the overall amount of US funding for family planning. This chapter also reports trends in US funding for family planning and reproductive health services, and it examines the relative size of that funding in relation to all global health funding—the pot of money at stake with the expanded version of the global gag rule. Detailed evidence from qualitative studies reviewed in this chapter indicate that the restrictions on US family-planning assistance under George W. Bush beginning in 2001 caused major disruptions in service delivery on the ground, especially in sub-Saharan Africa. This evidence is crucial for understanding the channels through which women's reproductive health outcomes are related to restrictions on US foreign aid.

How did family planning become included in US foreign policy in the first place? Chapter 3 places the global gag rule into a broader context by examining the longer-term history and objectives of US foreign aid for family planning. This history is filled with ironies and controversies, which may not be surprising given that the financial assistance relates to sex, contraception, and abortion. Family-planning assistance has taken place within a framework of global reproductive governance that is characterized by three distinct paradigms: population control, safe motherhood, and women's reproductive health. Early proponents of family-planning assistance beginning in the 1950s were motivated primarily by fears of a Malthusian catastrophe in which explosive population growth in developing countries in the face of limited natural resources would lead to widespread food shortages, environmental degradation, and macroeconomic crisis. The answer, it appeared, was to disseminate modern contraceptive techniques as widely as possible across large populations to reduce fertility rates and control population growth. By the late 1980s, as the predictions of Malthusian-type disasters failed to materialize and medical practitioners, scholars, and advocates around the world became more alarmed about high rates of maternal mortality, the paradigm surrounding population assistance shifted to safe motherhood. Growing pressure from feminists and women's groups to focus on the rights of all women and not just mothers contributed to the third paradigm shift in the 1990s toward women's reproductive health. Each time the United States has imposed the global gag rule, it has antagonized not only the global health providers who depend on US financial assistance to help fund their operations, but also the major donors, agencies, and governments who have carefully set the priorities and objectives of these paradigms in reproductive governance.

Having explored the history behind family-planning programs in developing countries, Chapter 4 examines their effectiveness in providing women with contraceptive access and reducing fertility. How contraceptive access affects women's fertility is less straightforward than it may seem. For this reason, the chapter uses an analysis of aggregate data, a theoretical model, and a review of the empirical literature to examine the relationship between contraceptive availability and fertility. A correlation analysis of the aggregate data clearly shows that as contraceptive use rises, fertility rates fall. In a similar vein, as the unmet need for contraception decreases, total fertility rates fall, thus supporting the main rationale for investments in family-planning programs. The effectiveness of family-planning programs is in fact the subject of numerous published studies, many of which have pointed to beneficial effects that include increased contraceptive usage and lower fertility. These aggregate data on contraception and fertility are consistent with a theoretical model of the factors that influence women's reproductive health decisions. The model can be used to predict the effects of an increase in the cost of contraceptives as might occur under the global gag rule. An increase in the price and a decline in availability of contraceptives are predicted to decrease the intensity with which women use contraception, which results in a higher risk of unintended pregnancies. Depending on the relative costs of having an abortion and giving birth, more unintended pregnancies will lead to higher abortion rates or birth rates or both.

An examination of the links between family planning and women's decision-making around fertility is incomplete without a clear understanding of the legal context in which women make these decisions. Chapter 5 provides a closer look at this issue with a detailed examination of global abortion laws and aggregate data on abortion rates. Not only have policies and practices around abortion existed since ancient times, they have evolved in ways that vary considerably across geographical regions according to deeply entrenched religious views, political ideologies, patriarchal structures, and strong stigmas. Although aggregate abortion rates have fallen globally since 1990, most of this decrease has occurred in wealthy countries, and they have actually risen in Africa and Latin America, where abortion laws are the most restrictive in the world. In fact, there is no evidence showing that legal restrictions lead to lower abortion rates. A critical conclusion from existing evidence is that instead of reducing abortion rates, restrictive laws change the conditions under which women obtain abortions in ways that involve greater risk to their health and safety. Unsafe abortion is one of the leading causes of maternal mortality, especially in Latin America and the Caribbean, where it causes a higher proportion of maternal deaths than other complications from pregnancy and birth. Given high rates of unsafe abortion and pressure from the international health community, some governments have started to liberalize their abortion laws. However, implementation has often been slow due to weak health infrastructure and fear of reprisal among providers and patients. Offsetting these challenges are innovations in reproductive health technologies that have made it possible for women in some countries to have what is called a "medical abortion" using pharmaceuticals made available through the internet, pharmacies, and the black market. Although some consider medical abortion the next frontier in safe abortion, plenty of obstacles remain that prevent women from utilizing this option, including affordability, import restrictions, lack of information about proper usage, and slow-to-change stigmas around abortion.

Chapter 6 offers new econometric estimates of the impact of the global gag rule on abortion rates. The analysis employs a "difference in difference" strategy developed in Bendavid et al. (2011) that identifies the impact of the global gag rule as the difference in abortion rates before and after the 2001 policy reinstatement and the difference between countries with high and low exposure to the US policy. Abortion rates are constructed using Demographic and Health Survey data from 51 developing countries across four developing regions: sub-Saharan Africa, Latin America and the Caribbean, Eastern Europe and Central Asia, and South and Southeast Asia. The data set, which covers about 6.3 million woman-year observations from 1994 to 2008, also includes information about the women's education, marital status, age, and whether they live in an urban or rural setting. Merged into this extremely large data set are country-level indicators representing other factors that could determine women's decisions to have an abortion, including the country's life expectancy, contraceptive prevalence, abortion legislation, and other non-US sources of family-planning assistance.

Results from logistic regressions indicate that the global gag rule is associated with a very large increase in the likelihood of women getting an abortion in Latin America and the Caribbean. In this region, women in countries that were highly exposed to the global gag rule had more than three times the odds of having an abortion after the global gag rule was reinstated in 2001 compared to women in less-exposed countries before the reinstatement of the policy. The effect is also large for sub-Saharan Africa, where women in highly exposed countries had about twice the odds of having an abortion after the 2001 reinstatement of the policy compared to women in less exposed countries before the policy was reinstated. Abortion rates rose in both these regions despite their very restrictive legal regimes around abortion. In Eastern Europe and Central Asia, the odds of women seeking an abortion in high-exposure countries after the 2001 reinstatement did fall, but this effect was counterbalanced by increased odds of getting an abortion associated with family-planning assistance from other donors. Only in South and Southeast Asia did the policy appear to reduce abortion rates. Results also point to the lack of a conclusive and consistent relationship between strict abortion laws and women's likelihood of having an abortion. Hence in the majority of developing countries exposed to the global gag rule, the policy failed to achieve its objective of discouraging women from getting an abortion.

Chapter 7 concludes by highlighting the three biggest messages from the analysis presented in this book: (1) the global gag rule has failed to achieve its goal of reducing abortions; (2) restrictive legislation is associated with more unsafe abortions; and (3) the expanded global gag rule is likely to have negative repercussions across a range of health outcomes for women, children, and men. They are simple but powerful messages that should be heard by policymakers over the voices calling for an ideologically based policy that fails to achieve its desired outcome. The book closes with a more constructive and cost-effective approach for US family-planning assistance that targets integrated reproductive health services.

NOTE

1. This quotation was obtained from an interview I conducted on December 1, 2017, in New York City with Barbara Crane, a former official at Ipas (a global NGO that helps women access reproductive health services).

Chapter 2

Global Gag Rule

Politics and Scope

In 1984 at the International Conference on Population in Mexico City, the US delegation announced a major change in the allocation of US family-planning assistance abroad. This announcement reflected the antiabortion platform of President Ronald Reagan's election campaign and concerted efforts of the US antiabortion movement to extend its objectives to the rest of the world. Officially known as the Mexico City Policy, the policy prevents international NGOs from receiving family-planning aid, technical assistance, and contraceptive supplies from the United States if they perform or actively promote abortions as an option for family planning. Such NGOs include not only direct service providers (hospitals and clinics) but also reproductive health organizations, women's groups, and health research centers. In order to receive family-planning assistance from the United States, international NGOs are required to sign an official affidavit stating they will not perform abortions or provide abortion-related services (such as counseling, education, referrals, or training). If they do not comply, they are denied all family-planning assistance from the United States.

Because foreign NGOs had already been banned in the 1973 Helms Amendment from using US foreign aid to perform abortions as a method of family planning, the Mexico City Policy actually prevents NGOs from using their own funding to perform or promote abortions if they want to continue to receive assistance from the United States. Moreover, the Mexico City Policy also bans NGOs that receive US family-planning assistance from lobbying for the liberalization of abortion laws in the countries where they are based, a provision that affects a large number of developing countries where access to abortion is highly regulated. Because of the restrictions on healthcare providers from counseling their patients on abortion and from advocating for legal reforms, the Mexico City Policy was seen as stifling free speech, and it soon earned the more derisive name of the "global gag rule."

The global gag rule does have some exemptions. The funding restriction does not apply to foreign governments (national or subnational), multilateral agencies, or to public international organizations. If a foreign government or a public-sector organization abroad does perform abortions as a method of family planning or provides abortion counseling or referrals, then that organization must keep the US family-planning assistance in a segregated account that is not used for these services. The global gag rule also does not apply to US nonprofit organizations, which can continue to perform abortions and provide abortion counseling and referrals in the United States without losing financial assistance as long as they ensure that their foreign NGO partners are complying with the global gag rule requirements. There are also exemptions for some types of abortion-related services that foreign NGOs can still provide. These exemptions include postabortion care services to treat complications and injuries caused by legal or illegal abortions, as well as the provision of emergency contraception pills and counseling. Foreign NGOs do not lose their eligibility for US family-planning assistance if they perform abortions or provide abortion-related services in cases of rape, incest, or to save the life of the mother if her life would otherwise be endangered by carrying the fetus to term. Abortion counseling and referrals are also permitted in narrowly defined circumstances in which a pregnant woman living in a country where abortion is legal has already decided to have an abortion and she asks the service provider where she can obtain a safe abortion.

HISTORY AND TIMELINE OF THE GLOBAL GAG RULE

The Mexico City Policy is an extension of the 1973 Helms Amendment, which prohibits any foreign organization from using US funds to perform abortions as a method of family planning. The Helms Amendment in turn is an amendment of the US Foreign Assistance Act, which Congress passed in 1961 to separate the distribution of economic and development assistance from military aid. The Foreign Assistance Act also formally established a new independent agency—the US Agency for International Development (USAID)—to administer economic assistance and, more broadly, to fight global poverty and support democratic societies. The act also authorized USAID to conduct research on issues in global family planning and population, and the agency implemented its first family-planning program just four years later. By the late 1960s USAID had become one of the major players among other agencies and donor organizations in the global distribution of contraceptives, and it has remained the primary US agency on family planning and reproductive health (Kaiser Family Foundation, 2017b).

In the early years, officials at USAID believed that methods for terminating pregnancies in the early stages constituted an important part of effective family-planning services, and USAID allocated considerable funding toward research on technologies for performing abortions (Crane, 1994). However, not all groups in the United States supported USAID's objectives, with most opposition coming from the antiabortion movement, led by the Christian Right. Groups such as the Family Research Council, Concerned Women for America, Priests for Life, and Focus on the Family played strong roles in shaping the antiabortion platform and pressuring lawmakers to adopt antiabortion policies at the national and international levels (Gezinski, 2012). This pressure contributed to Congress's decision to approve the Helms Amendment, which prohibited USAID from using any government money for abortion-related activities except for research. Even when the global gag rule is not in effect, the Helms Amendment continues to constrain NGOs and healthcare providers in developing countries in their access to US financial assistance for abortion services.

The Christian Right and other socially conservative groups formed a powerful coalition that backed the election of Ronald Reagan as president in 1981. Early into his presidency, the Reagan administration adopted a more aggressive antiabortion policy stance, in part to appease the antiabortion groups that had been instrumental in Reagan's successful campaign for election. The administration's resolve to pursue antiabortion policies was reflected in a draft position paper that the White House Office of Policy Development prepared for the Second International Conference on Population, to be held in Mexico City in August 1984. The draft paper was leaked to the press shortly before the conference, generating heated debate within the government and also in the media about the proposed restrictions on US family-planning assistance. Not only did the policy document signal a new antiabortion position, it also announced the administration's profound departure from previous official statements on population policy. Family-planning programs would no longer constitute a crucial tool for reducing fertility abroad and promoting economic development. Rather, the US government now viewed market-oriented reforms and government deregulation in developing countries as the key policy strategy for promoting economic growth and lifting countries out of poverty (Dixon-Mueller, 1993). Despite anger by critics, the final draft of the policy statement released by the White House and officially presented at the Mexico City conference did not budge from the administration's hardline policy stance against abortion. In fact, it further tightened the restrictions already in place on the use of USAID funds to pay for the performance of abortions as a family-planning method (White House Office of Policy Development, 1984).

In contrast to the First International Conference on Population in Bucharest in 1974, when most country delegations avoided discussing abortion and the resulting plan of action barely mentioned abortion, this issue took on more prominence at the 1984 conference in Mexico City (Crane, 1994). At the 1984 conference, the US delegation surprised and antagonized most countries by formally announcing its new position on abortion and population control in what became known as the Mexico City Policy. The US delegation aligned itself with the Vatican in an official statement that abortion should not be promoted as a family-planning method. With the exception of Iran, Libya, Syria, and Sudan, no developing countries supported the statement (Gezinski, 2012). The following excerpt from the policy objectives section of the official US policy statement is indicative of the stance taken by the Reagan administration:

> US support for family planning programs is based on respect for human life, enhancement of human dignity, and strengthening

of the family. Attempts to use abortion, involuntary sterilization, or other coercive measures in family planning must be shunned, whether exercised against families within a society or against nations within the family of man. . . . The United States does not consider abortion an acceptable element of family planning programs and will no longer contribute to those of which it is a part. (White House Office of Policy Development, 1984, 578)

The official statement also assured that the US government would immediately begin to implement the new policy in its negotiations on family-planning assistance with recipient organizations. The US policy represented a much stronger position against funding for abortion services, and it used language that characterized access to contraception as a matter of maternal and family health rather than women's reproductive and sexual health. Moreover, not only did the policy reflect the powerful influence of the antiabortion lobby in the United States, it also demonstrated a strong adherence to the types of neoliberal economic reforms that had started to dominate scholarly and policy discourse on economic development (Dixon-Mueller, 1993).

As shown in Figure 2.1, the global gag rule lasted five years, through the remainder of Reagan's presidency and another four years under George H. W. Bush, until it was rescinded by newly elected Democratic president Bill Clinton in 1993.[1] In his official memorandum revoking the policy, Clinton wrote that the antiabortion conditions on USAID family-planning assistance were excessively broad and unjustified, and that these conditions were not contained in the Foreign Assistance Act or any other US legislation. He further said that the conditions "have undermined efforts to promote safe and efficacious family planning programs in foreign nations" (Clinton, 1993, 216). The global gag rule did not get reinstated again for another eight years, when Republican President George W. Bush started his first of two four-year terms in 2001. However, during Bill Clinton's eight-year presidency, the Republican-controlled House of Representatives made numerous attempts in congressional negotiations to prevent the release of family-planning assistance. The Republicans succeeded in 1999, when they forced Bill Clinton to accept a modified version of the global gag rule in exchange for an agreement to authorize

Ronald Reagan	1981	
	1984	> Global gag rule introduced in Mexico City by Reagan administration
George H.W. Bush	1989	
Bill Clinton	1993	> Global gag rule rescinded by Clinton administration
	1999	> Modified gag rule in place due to political negotiations
	2000	> Modified gag rule dropped
George W. Bush	2001	> Global gag rule reinstated by Bush administration
Barack Obama	2009	> Global gag rule rescinded by Obama administration
Donald Trump	2017	> Global gag rule reinstated and extended by Trump administration

Figure 2.1 Timeline of the Global Gag Rule

Source: Adapted from Barot and Cohen (2015).

a $1 billion payment to the United Nations for back dues (Barot and Cohen, 2015). This modified version was in effect for just one year and then dropped.

President George W. Bush reinstated the global gag rule as a presidential executive order in 2001, and it remained in place through both of his terms of office. Justifying his official decision, Bush wrote, "It is my conviction that taxpayer funds should not be used to pay for abortions or advocate or actively promote abortion, either here or abroad" (Bush, 2001, 209). Bush also extended the policy coverage from USAID grant awards to voluntary population planning assistance from the US Department of State. In January 2009, newly elected Democratic president Barack Obama rescinded the policy, using language similar to Bill Clinton's in saying, "These excessively broad conditions on grants and assistance awards are unwarranted" (Obama, 2009, 215). The pendulum swung back again when President Donald Trump reinstated the gag in 2017. His policy directive, however, explicitly extended the coverage from just family-planning assistance to other types of global health assistance by calling on the government to "extend the requirements of the reinstated Memorandum to global health assistance furnished by all departments or agencies" (Trump, 2017, 188). Before this expansion, NGOs could still receive other types of US funding for global health, such as HIV/AIDS assistance, even if they were ineligible to receive family-planning assistance. However, as of January 2017, any NGO that refuses the conditions of the Mexico City Policy will no longer receive other kinds of global health funding from the United States. Renamed by the Trump administration as Protecting Life in Global Health Assistance, the expanded policy applies to all global health assistance that is appropriated under USAID, the State Department, and the Department of Defense.

The more punitive version under Trump is consistent with his administration's move to the right, and it also reflects the shift in US abortion politics toward the encroachment of restrictions on women's access to abortions. Since 2010 there has been an enormous expansion of state-level policies that restrict abortion access for women in the United States. These policies include parental permission requirements, restrictions on public funding, Targeted Regulation of Abortion Provider (TRAP) laws that place burdensome requirements on abortion facilities and doctors, informed consent laws, and mandated postcounseling waiting periods. These policies have aimed to reduce both abortion demand and supply. The most common of the state-level restrictions are informed consent laws, which require that women receive a state-authored information packet about fetal development, risks of abortion, and alternatives to abortion. These packets often contain images of the fetus, a practice that is consistent with the strategy of antiabortion movements to use fetal images and depict fetuses as people in order to persuade women to avoid ending "innocent lives" (Petchesky, 1990).

Such laws have a wide reach: two-thirds of all women seeking an abortion in the United States live in states with informed consent laws. Notably, research in Daniels, Ferguson, Howard, and Roberti (2016) based on evaluations by a panel of medical experts found that many of the state-authored information packets that are routinely handed out as part of the informed consent process have medically inaccurate statements. For example, about one-third of all statements about fetal development—such as "the head has formed" at week 2 and "brain activity can be recorded" at week 4—are medically inaccurate. State-level TRAP laws have also been encroaching on the ability of women to get an abortion, to the point that in 2016 the US Supreme Court struck down TRAP laws in Texas that had forced doctors to have hospital admitting privileges and had mandated that abortion clinics meet requirements for surgical centers. These kinds of state-level restrictions are symptomatic of the strong pressures that antiabortion groups have placed on US lawmakers to restrict access to abortion at the national and international levels. Moreover, restrictions on access to abortion within the United States have disproportionately impacted low-income women and women of color (Petchesky, 1990), just as the global gag rule primarily targets women of color living in low-income countries in the global South. Even though, on the surface, state-level TRAP laws may seem far removed from the global gag rule, they originate from the same antiabortion platform, and they both target the women who can least afford the restrictions on their reproductive health.

FUNDING PATTERNS

From its inception in 1984, the global gag rule has restricted family-planning assistance to developing countries across different regions. Numerous reports and studies have focused on repercussions of the global gag rule for sub-Saharan Africa because this region has some of the highest fertility and poverty rates in the world, but the gag rule has also restricted family-planning assistance to other developing regions. To examine regional patterns in the flow of US family-planning assistance, this chapter uses the Creditor Reporting System of the Organization for Economic Cooperation and Development, one of the most comprehensive sources of data on international aid flows across donor and recipient countries (OECD, 2017). This database is used to create Figure 2.2, which shows total official development assistance for family planning from the United States to developing countries across regions starting in 1995 (the first year of available data) and ending in 2015 (the most recent year available). Data are for committed aid flows in millions of current US dollars to all developing countries in Africa, the Americas (Central America, South America, and the Caribbean), Asia, and Europe. Note that the OECD classifies in a separate regional category any funding for projects that involve multiple countries in two or more regions.

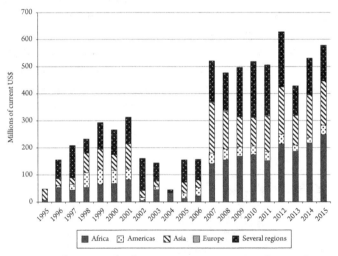

Figure 2.2 Total US Family-Planning Assistance to Developing Countries, 1995–2015

Note: Data represent total official development assistance from the United States for committed flows of family-planning assistance in millions of current US dollars. When commitments are for countries in more than one region, the OECD classifies those amounts in a separate aggregate for several regions.

Source: Constructed from data downloaded from the Creditor Reporting System, OECD (2017).

Figure 2.2 shows that total family-planning assistance declined substantially after the 2001 reinstatement of the global gag rule, from $312 million in 2001 to a low of just $44 million in 2004. US family-planning assistance has more than recovered since 2007, reaching a high point of $628 million in 2012 during the Obama presidency, when the gag rule was not in place. The figure shows that in 1995, most family-planning assistance went to Asian countries, and flows to Asia have surpassed those to sub-Saharan Africa in several subsequent years, especially from 2002 to 2006. That said, sub-Saharan Africa has consistently been the largest recipient region since 2008, absorbing anywhere from 30% to 43% of family-planning assistance from the United States. The actual shares are larger to the extent that the combined category of "several regions" includes sub-Saharan African countries as well. Transition economies in Central and Eastern Europe have received fairly little family-planning assistance from the United States over time, and the share going toward the Americas has remained at about 8% or less since 2007.

The extension of the 2017 global gag rule to other types of global health funding marks a turning point in US financial assistance. US global health funding comprises a number of important program areas, of which family-planning and reproductive health services are a fairly small proportion. Figure 2.3 shows that as of 2016, funding for HIV/AIDS constitutes

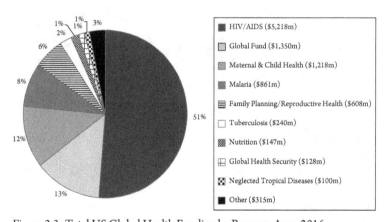

Figure 2.3 Total US Global Health Funding by Program Area, 2016
Note: Total global health funding in 2016 amounts to $10.2 billion.
Source: Reconstructed from data used in Figure 9 in Kaiser Family Foundation (2017b, 24).

the largest program area, accounting for 51% of a total of $10.2 billion in US global health funding. The Global Fund—an independent multilateral institution that finances HIV/AIDS, tuberculosis, and malaria programs in developing countries and receives more money from the United States than any other country—accounts for another 13% of US global health funding, followed closely by funding to promote maternal and child health and to fight malaria. Assistance for family planning and reproductive health comprises just 6% of US global health funding, but it is this slice of the pie that garners the most media attention and public scrutiny in the United States because of the abortion issue. Smaller amounts go toward fighting tuberculosis and various tropical diseases, and toward improving nutrition and global health security.

Consistent with the adage that the devil is in the details, the 2017 policy directive that expanded the global gag rule simultaneously kept intact the previous exemption for public international organizations and multilateral agencies (Kaiser Family Foundation, 2017a). By 2016, about 80% of total US global health funding was allocated to bilateral programs, with the remaining 20% going to multilateral institutions (mostly to the Global Fund, followed by Gavi, the vaccine alliance that supports immunization programs in low-income countries). The continued exemption of multilateral institutions means that the Global Fund and Gavi will not face funding cuts as a result of the expanded gag rule, and it means that press reports early in 2017 of more than $10 billion in US aid affected by the Trump policy were exaggerated. Subsequent reports in 2017 estimated the total amount of global health funding subject to cuts to be closer to $8 to 9 billion (Crane, Daulaire, and Ezeh, 2017).

In 2016, the year before the expanded gag rule was announced, the United States extended bilateral global health assistance to a total of 64 countries, just over half of which were in sub-Saharan Africa. Analysis in Kates and Moss (2017) indicates that among this group of countries, 37 had national abortion laws that were more liberal than the exemptions specified in the Mexico City Policy, with 22 of those countries in sub-Saharan Africa. In other words, while the US rule does allow NGOs abroad to perform abortions with their own funding when the woman's life is in danger or in cases of rape and incest, 37 countries had national abortion laws that specified additional grounds upon which women could have an abortion—usually to preserve the woman's physical health and in cases of debilitating fetal impairment. Under the conditions of the extended Mexico City Policy, NGOs in these 37 countries will no longer be allowed to provide legal abortions using their own funds for these additional grounds if they want to keep receiving US financial assistance. Hence compliance by NGOs with the expanded global gag rule can reduce the availability of legal abortion services in 37 developing countries, most of them in sub-Saharan Africa. The other 27 countries have national abortion laws that are even more restrictive than the Mexico City Policy. In that case the United States will not impact the provision of legal abortion services, but it will still restrict other abortion-related activities such as counseling and legal advocacy efforts (Kates and Moss, 2017).

The extended global gag rule will impact US funding from additional government agencies besides USAID. Until 2003, USAID was the largest agency responsible for global health funding. Over time its main objectives in family-planning and reproductive health services have evolved from focusing mostly on stabilizing population growth toward greater emphasis on reducing high-risk pregnancies, extending birth intervals, preventing HIV transmission through education and provision of condoms, and supporting women's rights. In 2003, President George W. Bush announced the PEPFAR program—the President's Emergency Plan for AIDS Relief—in response to the global AIDS epidemic. The US State Department was tasked with funding PEPFAR, making it the largest US agency responsible for global health funding after 2003. By 2016, the State Department disbursed 59% of a total of $10.2 billion in US global health funding, followed by USAID (30%) and the Department of Health and Human Services (11%) (Kaiser Family Foundation, 2017b). Although USAID is technically still an independent agency, the lines between USAID and the State Department became blurred in a major reorganization in 2006 when President George W. Bush appointed an ambassador to hold two positions concurrently across these units: the administrator of USAID and the director of US Foreign Assistance at the State Department.

The PEPFAR program is the main reason why US funding for HIV/AIDS currently dominates over other global health programs and has done so for at least the past 10 years. As shown in Figure 2.4,

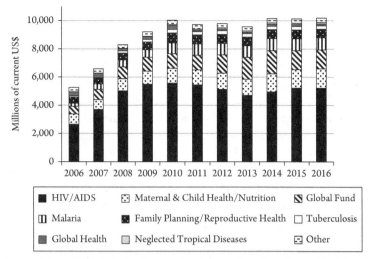

Figure 2.4 US Global Health Funding by Program Area Over Time, 2006–2016
Source: Reconstructed from data used in Figure 8 in Kaiser Family Foundation (2017b, 24).

already in 2006 funding for HIV/AIDS comprised half of global health funding, and that share actually reached more than 60% just two years later before settling back down to one-half. The percentages for the other categories of global health have been quite stable over the past decade, with maternal and child health, the Global Fund, and malaria constituting the largest health programs after HIV/AIDS. Funding for malaria was boosted by another program announced during the George W. Bush administration, the President's Malaria Initiative (PMI). The allocation for family planning and reproductive health has also remained fairly constant since 2006 at about 6% to 8%. Interestingly, the total amount of global health funding almost doubled between 2006 and 2010 (from $5.3 billion to 10.0 billion) under the Republican administration of George W. Bush and then the Democratic administration of Barack Obama. Total funding has since remained at about $10 billion, at least until 2016. Trump's threatened cuts to global health funding in 2017 would constitute a major reversal relative to the growth seen in the past 10 years that was initiated and sustained by both Republican and Democratic administrations.

DEFUNDING THE UNITED NATIONS POPULATION FUND

While most discourse around US foreign aid for family planning has centered on the global gag rule, a second controversy around international family-planning assistance involves similar issues but has attracted less attention. Specifically, the US government has alternately funded and defunded the United Nations Population Fund (UNFPA) in essentially the same pattern as the alternating rescission and reinstatement of the global gag rule. The UNFPA is the main organization in the United Nations that assists developing countries with population issues through research, training, and advising. It has its roots as a trust fund that was created in 1967 before becoming a subsidiary of the UN General Assembly in 1969. As a founding member of the UNFPA, the US government was required to make an annual contribution. By 1973 the annual budget of the UNFPA was $52 million, with the US funding at least half of that amount (Robinson, 2010).

A decade later, the Republican Party leadership had turned against the mission of the agency, and pressure mounted to end US financial support. The Helms Amendment already prevented the UNFPA from directly providing abortion services, but antiabortion advocates wanted to withhold US funding from the UNFPA altogether. In 1985 Congress passed the Kemp-Kasten Amendment, an amendment to appropriations legislation that prevents US foreign aid from being allocated to any organization that the president deems is supporting or participating in involuntary sterilization or coercive abortion practices. The Reagan administration subsequently accused UNFPA of being complicit in coercive abortion practices because of its presence in China, a country with an extremely strict one-child policy (Barot and Cohen, 2015). Ronald Reagan used this new amendment and the China rationale to withhold the entire US contribution (a total of $36 million) from the UNFPA the following year. Although this amount was relatively small compared to the total US bilateral assistance for family planning, it still constituted a large portion of the UNFPA budget.

The Kemp-Kasten Amendment must be renewed every year, and it has remained in effect to the current day. Unlike the global gag rule, which applies only to international NGOs, the Kemp-Kasten Amendment also applies to multilateral organizations and NGOs based in the United States. Thus far the UNFPA has been the largest organization impacted by funding cuts through this piece of legislation. Since the Kemp-Kasten Amendment was first passed by Congress in 1985, the defunding and funding of the UNFPA has effectively followed the same pattern as the global gag rule, with Republican presidents defunding the agency and Democratic presidents restoring and even increasing the funding to UNFPA. At issue is the extent to which a president interprets the organization's support for, or participation in, programs of involuntary sterilization or coercive abortion. Republican presidents have interpreted even indirect support and participation as being subject to the Kemp-Kasten Amendment, while Democratic presidents have determined that only direct support and participation warrant a denial of funding. In January 2017 the Trump administration invoked the Kemp-Kasten Amendment to again defund UNFPA.

IMPACTS OF THE GLOBAL GAG RULE ON REPRODUCTIVE HEALTH SERVICES

In principle, the global gag rule operates through several channels in its impact on reproductive health services provided by NGOs that receive family-planning assistance from USAID.[2] First, organizations that do not comply with the global gag rule and stand by their missions of providing complete reproductive health services—including abortion procedures, counseling, and referrals—will lose USAID funding. In this case there are two possible scenarios: (1) the organizations may be forced to close if funding from USAID comprises a large share of their total funding and if they cannot make up the shortfall from other donations, or (2) the organizations continue to provide complete services at potentially reduced capacity depending on the amount of the funding shortfall and the extent to which new donations offset the USAID cuts. The second major channel through which the global gag rule operates is organizations that decide to comply with the policy in order to retain their US funding. In this case the services that are offered to women are less comprehensive and exclude abortion procedures and counseling. Any reductions in reproductive health services could, in turn, lead to the unintended consequence of higher abortion rates if family-planning services and contraceptive supplies act as substitutes for abortion in preventing unwanted births.

The US policy may not impact total family-planning assistance to developing countries very much because the US funds could be redirected toward NGOs that do not perform or promote abortions. US funds could also be redirected toward foreign governments, which are exempt from the global gag rule (Asiedu, Nanivazo, and Nkusu, 2013). Moreover, other donor countries could step in and increase their own contributions to make up for the US shortfall. For example, a Dutch-led campaign launched in February 2017 quickly led to several hundred million dollars in committed donations (Crane et al., 2017). However, it is unlikely that other donors will be able to completely fill the gap. Evidence in Asiedu et al. (2013) indicates that the US policy in previous Republican administrations led to a 3%–6% reduction in total family-planning assistance from all donor countries while the policy was in effect, and countries with high fertility rates were more susceptible to the cuts. Moreover, when other governments have stepped in to partially cover the US funding cuts, their additional funding only covered family-planning assistance. This time all global health funding, which is a much larger amount (up to $10 billion), is at stake.

When it was first implemented in 1984 and reinstated again in 2001, the global gag rule generated heated debate within and outside of the United States, but there was very little systematic evidence at the time on the consequences of the policy for reproductive health services and abortion rates. We do know that the introduction of the global gag rule in 1984 and its reinstatement in 2001 had an immediate budgetary impact on the world's largest family-planning NGO—the International Planned Parenthood Federation (IPPF), but it is not clear how the funding cut affected the actual provision of services by its affiliates. IPPF was founded in 1952 with a mission to provide family-planning and reproductive health services and education. With funding from multiple governments and large private donors, IPPF has expanded over the years to about 60 million people in over 170 countries annually, operating through 160 member associations (IPPF, 2015). It is also a major lobbyist for legal reforms that give individuals more choice in family planning, including legal access to abortions.

In 1984, after having supported IPPF for 17 years, USAID withdrew its aid commitment when IPPF refused to comply with the global gag rule (Camp, 1987). IPPF's decision to refuse the terms of the global gag rule was not an easy decision to make. The funding cut amounted to $11 million, which at the time constituted almost 25% of IPPF's operating budget. Initially during the negotiations, USAID officials stated that IPPF would continue to receive financial assistance as long as it stopped using its main budget to pay for abortion activities, which amounted to about $500,000 per year. IPPF administrators signaled they would try to get this provision approved by the executive board. However, USAID subsequently strengthened the severity of the provision and demanded that IPPF also impose the antiabortion restriction on all of its independent national affiliates that were receiving grant funding from IPPF. Those affiliates would not even be allowed to use their own money to fund abortion activities if they wanted to keep receiving IPPF support. Because IPPF's charter prevented it from imposing such a policy on its affiliates, IPPF negotiators decided not to comply with USAID's requirements. Thus its grant from USAID expired at the end of 1984 without renewal. This course of events set the precedent for other large family-planning agencies: not only would they need to comply with the administration's antiabortion policies themselves, but so would their foreign affiliates (Camp, 1987). Many of these family-planning agencies, including Marie Stopes International (MSI), decided to not comply.[3]

As of 2001, only two formal studies had evaluated the impact of the first iteration of the global gag rule on the provision of family-planning services in developing countries (Cincotta and Crane, 2001). Both of these studies were qualitative in nature, based on interviews with family-planning providers that had agreed to comply with the conditions of the global gag rule. They focused on the direct impacts on funding and on services offered but did not attempt to estimate the impacts on fertility or abortion rates. The first study was based on site visits to foreign NGOs in 10 developing countries in 1987 and 1988. Preliminary results published in Camp (1987) indicate that of the 31 major agencies visited, about two-thirds had not been affected by the global gag rule that had been introduced in 1984, either because they were operating under cost-reimbursable contracts that were not subject to the conditions of the gag rule, or because their agreements with USAID had not come up for renewal.[4] Only six of the remaining agencies stated in their interviews that their agreement to comply with the restrictions of the policy would affect their operations. In most cases, though, it appears that the organizations had other options that would allow them to continue to work with service providers that might object to the abortion restrictions (Camp, 1987). Hence the evidence from this first study suggests that the impact of the 1984 global gag rule on the provision of family-planning services in the 10 countries that were visited was rather limited.

The second study on the consequences of the 1984 enactment of the global gag rule is based on interview data at 49 subproject sites in six developing countries (Blane and Friedman, 1990). The authors concluded that most of the subprojects visited had not been substantially affected by the global gag rule. However, the researchers did find problems with several of the subprojects that caused women to be denied services. These problems revolved around the health providers being overcautious in their interpretation of the policy restrictions to the extent that their fear of losing USAID funding caused them to deny clients services that were actually permitted under the policy. Examples cited in the report include the discontinuation of treatment for septic abortions; restrictions on research-related activities; notifications to physicians who worked at NGOs that they could not provide legal abortions at their own private practices when in reality they could; and the denial of appropriate medical care or counseling to clients in need. The authors concluded that these fear-based reactions on the part of healthcare providers may have affected women's health in some instances. Unfortunately it is hard to determine whether this experience was generalizable and how widespread these fear-based reactions were in affected countries.

Shortly after President Bush reinstated the global gag rule in 2001, a consortium of NGOs led by Population Action International (PAI) conducted a series of case studies based on site visits and interviews in several developing countries that had experienced restrictions on USAID funding. Overall, these case studies suggest that the 2001 reinstatement of the global gag rule had larger negative impacts on the provision of reproductive health services than the first iteration of the policy when it was introduced in 1984 (PAI, 2005). The PAI case studies indicate that the funding cuts beginning in 2001 resulted in clinic closures, fewer services, and reduced contraceptive supplies, which in turn affected not only family planning but also other health services such as prenatal and postnatal obstetric care, infant and child healthcare, immunizations, cervical cancer screening, malaria treatment, and screening and treatment for sexually transmitted infections including HIV/AIDS. This assessment is echoed in Crane and Dusenberry (2004), which argues that the 2001 reinstatement of the global gag rule was likely to have more detrimental repercussions than the first round of the gag rule, when relatively few NGOs were affected by the conditions of the policy.

The PAI (2005) summary report indicates that by 2002, USAID had halted all supply shipments of donated contraceptives from the United States to leading family-planning associations in 16 countries. All of these associations were affiliates of the IPPF, and they were the only organizations within their respective countries slated to receive the donated contraceptives. Family-planning associations in another 13 countries that were not affiliated with the IPPF but still chose to defy the global gag rule also lost their shipments of USAID-donated contraceptives. Two of the 29 countries experiencing disruptions to their in-kind assistance from USAID were Ethiopia and Lesotho. A rural clinic in Ethiopia that had refused to comply with the global gag rule reported that it stopped receiving USAID shipments of Depo-Provera, which was used by about 70% of its patients. The Lesotho Planned Parenthood Association—which had received not only Depo-Provera and IUDs but also close to half a million condoms between 1998 and 2000—was denied further shipments the following year when it refused to comply with the policy conditions.

The PAI (2005) summary report also indicates that in Kenya, two of the top family-planning organizations (the Family Planning Association of Kenya and Marie Stopes International Kenya) closed five of their clinics, cut staffing in the remaining clinics by up to 30%, and increased their fees in order to maintain operations. Two of the clinics that closed were located in large slum neighborhoods in the capital city with no public-sector clinics to take their place. In another one of the case study countries, the Planned Parenthood Association of Zambia (PPAZ)—the largest private family-planning organization in Zambia and the only NGO to provide clinical services—refused to comply with the reinstatement of the global gag rule in 2001 and thereby was denied USAID family-planning assistance, which had amounted to 24% of its total funding. Within four years, PPAZ lost 26 of its original 68 staff members and had to offer fewer reproductive health services due to the funding cuts and insufficient support from other donors to offset the cuts. For similar reasons the country lost the Zambia Integrated Health Program, a large project focusing on comprehensive family planning, HIV, and malaria services that had been funded by USAID (PAI, 2005).

Zimbabwe also experienced funding cuts. The Zimbabwe National Family Planning Council (ZNFPC), which had been established in 1985 with support from USAID, was one of the country's largest organizations to provide clinical family-planning services, sexual health education, and HIV/AIDS programs. The ZNFPC opted to comply with the 2001 global gag rule so it did not lose direct family-planning assistance from the United States. However, it also depended on assistance from the International Planned Parenthood Federation and on UNFPA, both of which experienced major losses due to Bush's reinstatement of the gag as well as the defunding of UNFPA. These international agencies were thus forced to reduce their financial support for the ZNFPC, which in turn prevented it from expanding its family-planning programs to meet the country's growing demand (PAI, 2005).

Besides losses in financial and in-kind assistance, another outcome of the global gag rule was the creation of inefficiencies due to the requirements that aid recipients not provide abortion services. The resulting separation of abortion-related services from other reproductive health services proved especially problematic in Romania, where abortion was legal and fairly common because the national health system compensated doctors more for abortion than for providing contraception. The PAI (2005) report concludes that by preventing the thorough integration of abortion services with contraceptive services and counseling, women who got abortions were not receiving adequate postabortion counseling and information on contraception. Hence the global gag rule, by failing to reduce unwanted pregnancies, made it more difficult for USAID, one of Romania's largest donors, to help Romania lower its abortion rate and decrease women's reliance on abortion as a method of family planning.

As a final example from the PAI case studies, Nepal also experienced disruptions to reproductive health services and supplies as a result of the 2001 reinstatement of the global gag rule. The largest NGO to provide family-planning services in Nepal—the Family Planning Association of Nepal (FPAN)—refused to comply with the conditions of the global gag rule. It lost $100,000 in annual funding that had supported three major clinics that provided comprehensive family-planning services to approximately 20,000 clients. Although increased funding from other donors helped to partially offset the shortfall, FPAN still had to let go of 60 doctors and nurses, and it changed to a fee-for-service business model in order to meet expenses. It also lost $400,000 worth of contraceptives from USAID, and it lost funding for its mobile reproductive health clinics in remote rural areas (PAI, 2005). Inefficiencies due to the separation of abortion-related services from contraceptive services were also documented in Nepal, as was confusion about changing policy requirements over time and excessive administrative burdens among aid recipients. In Nepal, not only providers but also patients were overburdened by the separation and sometimes denial of services caused by administrative requirements contained in the global gag rule (Taylor and Kumar, 2011).

ESTIMATED IMPACTS ON ABORTION RATES

Country case studies are a useful methodology to sort out questions about the transmission mechanism between foreign aid cuts and women's access to reproductive health services. However, while case studies are illustrative, they may not be representative of an entire country or region, and they often cannot demonstrate a direct link to changes in fertility and abortion rates. Statistical studies based on regression analysis using national surveys help to address this concern. That said, only two previously published studies have used regression analysis to estimate the impact of the global gag rule on fertility and abortion rates. The first, Jones (2015), uses individual-level data on induced abortions in Ghana and shows that the US policy contributed to more unintended pregnancies and more induced abortions. Note that the term *induced abortion* is often used synonymously with abortion and refers to the purposeful termination of a pregnancy. This action contrasts with a miscarriage, which refers to the spontaneous termination of a pregnancy.

In particular, before the global gag rule was reinstated by George W. Bush in 2001, NGOs in Ghana had been allocated almost $800,000 in USAID funding for family planning, with Planned Parenthood of Ghana (PPAG) scheduled to receive well over half of that amount. Within the next two years PPAG progressively lost this USAID funding, resulting in the closure or consolidation of numerous health clinics, mostly in rural areas. Jones estimates that PPAG was forced to close over half of its clinics, which amounts to a 12% total decline in patient access to all facilities given that PPAG served about one-fifth of the facility-based market for family planning. PPAG also lost in-kind donations of contraceptives, which contributed to reductions in stocks of modern contraceptive methods. In total, the clinic closures and contraceptive stock reductions led to a 10% reduction in the national supply of contraceptives, with larger reductions in rural areas than in urban areas.

Jones estimates that this reduced access to contraception resulted in a 10% increase in pregnancies among rural women, mostly because women were either not willing or not able to use traditional birth control methods to compensate for the decline in access to modern contraceptives. Women's responses to the increases in unplanned pregnancies varied by their wealth. The poorest women (in the lowest two wealth quintiles) did not have more abortions, largely because abortions in Ghana are very expensive. Wealthier women (in the upper three wealth quintiles), regardless of their education levels, used abortion to terminate 4 out of every 10 of the additional pregnancies. Hence in Ghana, the decreases in US financial assistance had the consequence of reduced access to contraception, more unplanned pregnancies, higher fertility rates, and more abortions. The most vulnerable segment of the population in a country that already had relatively high fertility and maternal mortality—rural Ghanaian women—bore the brunt of the burden of the US policy.

The second published study to use regression analysis in examining the impact of the global gag rule also finds that the restrictions on US family-planning assistance led to higher abortion rates in recipient countries. Bendavid, Avila, and Miller (2011) uses household-level data from the Demographic and Health Surveys (DHS) for 20 countries in sub-Saharan

Africa to calculate the likelihood of women seeking an induced abortion between 1994 and 2008. The analysis also uses data from the Creditor Reporting System of the OECD to calculate exposure to cuts in family-planning assistance from the United States. A country is considered to have high exposure to the global gag rule if US family-planning assistance per capita was higher than the median for the sample countries before the gag rule was reinstated in 2001, and, similarly, exposure is low if the country's US family-planning assistance per capita was below the sample median before 2001. These data are used to estimate a regression model that tests how the odds of seeking an induced abortion after 2001 differ between high-exposure and low-exposure countries.

The study finds that after the 2001 reinstatement, women living in countries that were highly exposed to family-planning assistance from USAID had more than twice the odds of having an induced abortion compared to before 2001 and compared to women living in countries that were less exposed to US family-planning assistance. This estimate controls for various characteristics that could also affect the likelihood of women getting an abortion, including the women's age, marital status, education, and urban versus rural residence, as well several country-level characteristics. The main explanation for these results is that the supply of contraception could not keep up with demand, so women substituted abortion for contraception. Even though the prevalence of modern contraceptive use continued to rise over time across countries in the sub-Saharan African sample, it rose more slowly in the high-exposure countries. Thus, as with the Jones (2015) analysis, this cross-country study for sub-Saharan Africa demonstrates that the second round of the global gag rule resulted in higher abortion rates.

CONCLUSION

Since its 1984 introduction, the Mexico City Policy—infamously known as the global gag rule—has evoked passionate debate and strong reactions within and outside of the United States. Proponents have claimed that the policy prevents US foreign aid from funding abortion services. Even though the 1973 Helms Amendment already prohibited foreign organizations from using US funds to perform abortions, proponents of the Mexico City Policy argue that money is fungible and the additional restrictions are needed to prevent US financial assistance from being used indirectly for abortion-related services and lobbying activities. Opponents have argued that the policy infringes on the rights of international NGOs by restricting how they use their own funding, and that it encroaches on their freedom of speech by prohibiting abortion-related counseling and lobbying efforts. They also assert that the global gag rule has caused major losses for NGOs abroad in terms of funding cuts and diminished capacity to provide comprehensive reproductive health services. As a result, women seeking abortion services have had to use lower-quality services from the government or from inadequately funded private providers. In worst-case scenarios, women with unplanned pregnancies have resorted to unsafe providers or to self-induced abortion (Cincotta and Crane, 2001).

Until fairly recently, the only systematic evidence on the impact of the global gag rule came from a number of country case studies based on interview data. Two of these case studies focus on the first iteration of the global gag rule in place from 1984 to 1992, and both find that the impact on the provision of reproductive health services in the sample countries appears to have been rather limited (Camp, 1987; Blane and Friedman, 1990). The interviews do reveal a problem with some healthcare providers being overcautious and denying services to clients that were actually permitted, but the magnitude of this problem is unclear. Another set of country case studies conducted by a consortium of NGOs shows that the second iteration of the global gag rule in place from 2001 to 2008 did indeed cause substantial reductions in reproductive health services and contraceptive supply shortages in the sample countries (PAI, 2005). Hence the reinstatement of the global gag rule in 2001 appears to have caused far greater disruption to reproductive health services than the introduction of the policy in 1984, most likely because the dependency on foreign aid in recipient countries had grown and because more NGOs refused to comply with the antiabortion conditions of US family-planning assistance after 2001.

These country case studies prove helpful in documenting the transmission mechanisms between US foreign aid restrictions and women's access to reproductive health services. However, while the case studies provide dramatic illustrations of how US funding cuts have led to clinic closures,

NGO staff reductions, and contraceptive supply shortages, they are based on qualitative data from a relatively small sample of service providers that were not randomly selected. Providing additional information, two statistical studies used large-scale survey data and regression analysis to demonstrate that the second iteration of the global gag rule caused abortion rates to rise in sub-Saharan Africa (Bendavid et al., 2011; Jones, 2015). The main channel through which the gag rule raised abortion rates was cutbacks in reproductive health services and contraceptive supplies. Given that NGOs in other developing regions also rely on US family-planning assistance to help meet the demand for reproductive health services, an important question is whether the key finding in these two quantitative studies for sub-Saharan Africa applies to other developing regions. More evidence is necessary in order to design effective foreign aid policy that does not have the unintended consequence of raising abortion rates and potentially harming women's health in developing countries.

NOTES

1. All the official policy documents associated with the announcement and the subsequent rescissions and reinstatements of the Mexico City Policy have been published in the journal *Population and Development Review* and are included in the bibliography as White House Office of Policy Development (1984), Clinton (1993), Bush (2001), Obama (2009), and Trump (2017).
2. This framework also applies to potential impacts from the broader cuts to all global health funding in the 2017 extended version of the global gag rule.
3. MSI, another large global family planning NGO, also refused to comply with the conditions of the global gag rule as a matter of principle, resulting in the discontinuation of family planning assistance from the United States. Founded in 1976, MSI provides contraceptive services and safe abortions to women in developing countries, and it lobbies governments for legal reforms that give women access to abortion. It has grown to provide services to 21 million women in 37 countries annually (MSI, 2015b). It is difficult to find evidence on the extent to which MSI relied on US funding in the 1980s when the global gag rule was introduced, but documentation for recent years indicates that USAID is the second largest donor of grant income after the United Kingdom's Department of International Development (MSI, 2015a).
4. The final results of this first study are contained in unpublished materials cited in Cincotta and Crane (2001).

Chapter 3

US Assistance for Family Planning

History and Objectives

The global gag rule affects women's reproductive health in developing countries due to the reliance of healthcare providers on US financial assistance for family-planning services. This chapter explores how the United States grew to become the world's largest donor country for family-planning programs abroad and how the objectives behind these aid flows have changed over time. The 2017 reinstatement of the global gag rule constitutes yet another shift in a long history of US government involvement in family-planning efforts, a history filled with ironies. As a case in point, the United States has become the dominant international source of financial assistance for family planning and reproductive health despite family planning being viewed in the United States as obscene during the 1800s. The antiabortion stance taken on by Republican administrations since the introduction of the global gag rule in 1984 is also ironic given that in the two decades preceding the gag rule, US strategies to support family planning in developing countries—led by prominent Republicans—featured abortion as a method of population control. Foreign policy related to promoting economic development abroad was not immune to powerful domestic pressure from the antiabortion lobby to control women's access to abortion.

How did the ideologies and politics around women's reproductive health come to fluctuate so much? To answer this question (which is the subject of a voluminous literature), this chapter highlights some of the key events, people, and institutions that shaped the progression of US assistance for family planning.[1] This discussion is situated in a framework of global reproductive governance, which refers to the process through which various historical agents—including governments, religious institutions, donor agencies, and nongovernmental organizations—used policies and programs, economic incentives, directives, and other forms of persuasion to manage and control women's reproductive behaviors (Morgan and Roberts, 2012). This global governance in family planning is defined by three successive paradigms: population control, safe motherhood, and women's reproductive health (Suh, 2017). The chapter also shows the extent to which developing countries depend on US financial assistance and other sources of finance for family-planning services.

POPULATION CONTROL

In the 1800s and early 1900s, contraception was viewed as obscene, and family planning was the object of antiobscenity laws. The Comstock Law, passed in 1873, prohibited trade in and circulation of erotica, contraceptives, and sex toys. People could even be punished for using the postal service to mail personal letters with sexual content. The law was named after Anthony Comstock, a salesman who felt deeply affronted by the prostitution and pornography he saw on the streets of New York City. Because he thought that contraception promoted lewd and lustful acts, he included contraception in his campaign to ban trade in obscene materials not only in the New York but across the nation. After the promulgation of Comstock's obscenity law, about half of all states also passed legislation banning prostitution and the possession of pornography and contraceptives.

The family-planning movement can be traced back to this inopportune time period and the advocacy of several key individuals in the birth control movement, especially Margaret Sanger and Marie Stopes. Margaret Sanger first gained public attention in 1914 when she faced legal sanction under the Comstock Law for her 1914 book *Family Limitation*, an instruction manual for family-planning techniques. Undaunted, she started the first birth control clinic in the United States just two years later. In 1921 she created the American Birth Control League, which later became the Planned Parenthood Federation of America. She spent the next few decades advocating for the legalization of contraception and fundraising for the development of new contraceptive methods. Across the Atlantic, writer and paleobotanist Marie Stopes started the first birth control clinic in Britain in 1921 and ultimately opened up a number of birth control clinics across the country. She also worked to raise awareness about birth control through her writing, which included a national newsletter. Both Sanger and Stopes believed strongly in women's rights, and they argued that women should be empowered with access to contraception so they could avoid unwanted pregnancies.

Efforts to develop new forms of birth control in the United States accelerated in the 1950s as birth control advocates, scholars, and population experts began to focus on the consequences of rapid world population growth in developing countries. They argued that high fertility rates in developing countries were the root cause of poverty, with unsustainable population growth inevitably leading to food shortages, environmental problems, unemployment, and homelessness. Underlying these concerns were the writings of British social philosopher Thomas Malthus dating back to the late 1700s. Malthus hypothesized that population growth—fueled by Europe's increasing prosperity during the Industrial Revolution—would outpace the growth of agricultural production, ultimately causing a catastrophe marked by famine and disease. This premise gained support during the 1950s, especially in the United States, as neo-Malthusian scholars, advocates, and policymakers blamed poverty in the developing world on excessive reproduction.

Fears about overpopulation in the face of scarce resources helped to mobilize support for population control programs in developing countries. The year 1952 marked the establishment of two major nonprofit organizations that focused on population control issues: the IPPF and the Population Council. IPPF, founded by Margaret Sanger's Planned Parenthood Federation of America and seven other family-planning organizations, provided family-planning and reproductive health services in developing countries. The Population Council, founded by John D. Rockefeller III, produced research on population growth, family-planning practices, and new fertility control methods. These organizations were subsequently joined by the Ford Foundation, the Rockefeller

Foundation, and Pathfinder International as they played leading roles in conducting research on population control and funding family-planning programs abroad.

Also in 1952, India was the first developing country to establish a population control program. Family-planning programs began to spread across developing countries as donors, governments, and scholars pushed for contraceptive-based approaches to control women's fertility. Their primary goal was to reduce population growth by distributing new contraceptive methods to large populations; empowering individual women to have reproductive choice and improving women's well-being was less of a policy priority (Sinding, 2007). The influential book *Population Growth and Economic Development* (Coale and Hoover, 1958) provided further rationale for large-scale population control programs as experts pointed to women's high fertility as a major barrier to modernization and economic growth. Another influential voice at this time was William Draper, an investment banker who chaired a committee to review foreign aid priorities for President Dwight D. Eisenhower. Although the final "Draper Report" urged the US government to prioritize population control in its development assistance, Eisenhower rejected the report's recommendation due to his concerns about opposition from the Catholic Church in regard to family planning (Goldberg, 2009).[2]

Around 1960, efforts to distribute contraceptives globally accelerated with the introduction of the birth control pill and the modern intrauterine device. By the mid-1960s the family-planning movement was in full swing after major international agencies started to contribute substantial funding for the provision of family-planning services. The US government was not a major player in this movement until 1965, when President Lyndon B. Johnson used his second State of the Union address to emphasize the importance of taking action to control population growth. Johnson said, "I will seek new ways to use our knowledge to help deal with the explosion in world population and the growing scarcity in world resources" (Johnson, 1965). Also in 1965, the Supreme Court took a major move to limit the scope of the Comstock Law by permitting married couples to use contraception.[3] Prompted by President Johnson's call to take action on population control, US policymakers became more involved in supporting family-planning programs both domestically and internationally. Adding to the impetus to take action were concerns that the imbalance between population size and the availability of natural resources, coupled with the transition in a number of developing countries from colonial rule to independence, would make countries more vulnerable to the spread of socialism. Lawmakers thus utilized financial assistance for population control in developing nations as a means to support US national security objectives and stabilize the global economic environment during the Cold War.

The USAID began its first population and reproductive health program in 1965. By 1968, USAID—with strong bipartisan support—had fully incorporated family planning into its foreign aid objectives and started purchasing and distributing condoms and other contraceptives in developing countries. Leading the organization was Reimert Ravenholt, a somewhat polarizing epidemiologist and professor who built up USAID's new population program from virtually no money and staff to become the world's largest source of population assistance within a decade.[4] Also in the late 1960s, the United States became one of the founding members of the UNFPA, largely because Republican president Richard Nixon and the US ambassador to the United Nations at the time, George H. W. Bush, wanted the United Nations to have an effective population control program. In fact, in a special message to Congress in 1969, Nixon identified population growth as "one of the most serious challenges to human destiny in the last third of this century" (Nixon, 1969). For the next 15 years or so, both Democratic and Republican administrations in the United States took the lead globally in trying to control rapid population growth by providing financial assistance for family-planning programs.

The 1968 publication of the best-selling book *The Population Bomb* by Paul Ehrlich helped to spread fear about overpopulation issues from policy and scholarly discourse to the general public, thus helping justify greater resources for population control programs. Several prominent news magazines, including *Time* and *Life*, featured cover stories on the problem of overpopulation. These publications placed additional pressure on US policymakers to become more involved in population control across the developing world, with substantial investments in the research, development, and dissemination of both contraceptive and abortion methods. USAID also channeled increasing amounts of money to organizations and agencies such as IPPF and UNFPA that offered family-planning services—including abortion—in developing countries. Not all scholars, however, were convinced that increasing the supply of contraceptives would reduce fertility. To help determine if there was indeed an unmet need for family planning, a number of surveys on knowledge, attitudes, and practices regarding family planning (which became known as the KAP surveys) were conducted across developing countries during the 1960s. Results from these surveys indicated that there was a gap between women's desires to control their fertility and their use of contraception. This documentation of a large number of women across the developing world who wanted to control their fertility and would use contraceptives if made available provided additional justification for governments and donors to invest in family-planning programs (Casterline and Sinding, 2000).

The early 1970s proved to be pivotal years in regard to US reproductive rights, abortion politics, and foreign aid for family planning. Working to refine vacuum aspiration techniques for abortion that had been developed in several other countries during the 1960s, US researchers developed a new device—the manual vacuum aspiration (MVA) syringe—to perform this type of abortion.[5] They approached Reimert Ravenholt at USAID with a prototype of this device, and after some further modifications USAID was actively funding the production and distribution of MVA technology. Also during this period, the Supreme Court made a landmark decision to legalize abortion in the United States. The Court's 1973 *Roe v. Wade* decision held that a woman has a constitutional right to obtain an abortion prior to fetal viability. However, incited by *Roe v. Wade*, conservative Christian groups and other members of the growing antiabortion movement in the United States pressured Congress to pass the Helms Amendment to the US Foreign Assistance Act. This amendment prohibited the use of US foreign assistance to pay for abortions as a method of family planning. The new legislation also prevented USAID from providing abortion services and manufacturing and distributing abortion devices in developing countries, so it turned to NGOs to engage in these activities. Since then, most population assistance from USAID has gone to NGOs such as IPPF and the International Pregnancy Advisory Service (Ipas). These NGOs in turn have worked with their global partners to help women across developing countries access family-planning and reproductive health services, including safe abortions.

Also in the early 1970s, the United Nations held its first world conference on population. To date, the UN has held three such conferences: the Bucharest World Population Conference in 1974, the Mexico City International Conference on Population in 1984, and the Cairo International Conference on Population and Development in 1994. The Bucharest conference stood out for its contentious negotiations between two coalitions and the strong influence that developing countries had in influencing the final outcome. One coalition, which was comprised of a number of high-income countries, including the United States, argued that rapid population growth constituted a major obstacle to economic development. According to this coalition, the key to solving the problem was targeted fertility control policies and programs. The second coalition, which consisted mostly of developing countries, argued that overpopulation was a result of slow economic development. This group accused high-income countries of supporting population control as a substitute for foreign aid, and coalition members argued that the solution to the problem of overpopulation was a new international economic order in which more resources would be distributed to developing countries. Conveying the view that fertility regulation would be unnecessary with greater financing for development, this coalition's slogan became "Economic development is the best contraceptive." Even though much of the conference wound up being devoted to ideological arguments about the structure of the international economic order rather than family-planning programs, delegates were able to agree upon a plan of action that emphasized the links between population, development, and the global economic system (Finkle and Crane, 1985).

This account of population control as the key to economic development would be incomplete without discussing the racialized, gendered, and class rationales that motivated early scholarship in population science and policies for family planning. This social context is often neglected in the demography and public health literature but frequently raised by feminist social scientists (Greenhalgh, 1996). Feminist critics argue that neo-Malthusian scholars and the reformers who adopted these overpopulation ideas were mostly concerned that the segment of the population growing too fast was "of the worst sort," and efforts were needed to "improve the race" in the undeveloped world through social reform as well as eugenic modification (Chowdhury, 2016). Family planning was seen as a method by which to limit the growth of biologically and socially inferior races. Moreover, Western hegemony would be preserved by controlling the wombs of women in developing country, thereby limiting the size and influence of the world's nonwhite population (Hodgson and Watkins, 1997).

This "gendered coloniality" underlying demographic scholarship and practice served to justify interventions into the reproductive lives of women living in the global South (McCann, 2016). These interventions included contraceptive experimentation and marketing. In their attempts to develop contraceptive methods that would work most effectively, scientists used poor women in Puerto Rico and Haiti as experimental subjects for Depo-Provera, high-dosage oral contraceptives, intrauterine devices, and various spermicides (Briggs, 2002; Petchesky, 1990). Some feminists claimed that USAID and contraceptive manufacturers used developing countries to unethically dump contraceptives considered unsafe for Western women (Hodgson and Watkins, 1997). Because the top priority of family-planning programs was to control population growth rather than address women's reproductive health needs, side effects and failure rates of particular methods mattered less than increasing contraceptive prevalence. Although the bodies of brown and black women became the direct subject of US foreign policy, policymakers had less concern for their reproductive rights (Chowdhury, 2016).

During the 1970s and 1980s, international funding for family planning tripled, and by the mid-1990s, 115 countries around the globe had large family-planning programs. As family-planning programs expanded across developing countries, contraceptive prevalence increased from less than 10% of women of reproductive age to about 60%, and fertility rates declined by more than half (Cleland et al., 2006). Often, in response to donor preferences for maximum aid effectiveness and accountability, these programs were run by independent bodies at arm's length from other government agencies. A growing number of industrial countries and development banks stepped in to fund family-planning programs while at the same time pressuring governments in developing countries to pass population policies and adopt family-planning programs. During this period, US funding for population assistance amounted to more than half of the total assistance globally (Sinding, 2007). However, other dimensions of women's health services—including prenatal care, postnatal care, safe abortion services, adequate staffing, and STD testing and treatment—received less attention. Family-planning programs thus attracted growing criticism among feminists and women's rights groups who favored a more comprehensive approach to women's reproductive health.

USAID continued to provide contraceptives and support family-planning programs abroad, subject to the constraints imposed by the 1973 Helms Amendment. During the 1970s it sponsored new projects and introduced localized distribution systems that delivered educational materials and family-planning services door-to-door (USAID, 2017). However, in the early 1980s, Ronald Reagan's administration extended the USAID restrictions of the Helms Amendment to abortion-related research, so USAID ended its funding of research on abortion technologies and also stopped training health practitioners abroad in abortion methods. By 1984, the US government no longer considered population control abroad to be a matter of national security, and it ceased emphasizing family-planning programs as a strategy to promote economic development. Instead, the US government began to advocate for deregulation and market-oriented reforms in poor countries as a means toward economic development and lower fertility. The government also took a stronger stance against US funding for abortion services.

As discussed in detail in the previous chapter, US officials formally announced this new position on population control and abortion at the 1984 International Conference on Population in Mexico City, instigating yet another contentious set of deliberations among UN member countries. The United States was more responsible than any other country for the politicization of the Mexico City conference (Finkle and Crane, 1985). Not only did the geographical proximity of the conference to the United States allow it to send an unusually large delegation to the conference, the United States also used its status as the world's biggest donor for population assistance to push its policy position. As noted in Finkle and Crane (1985, 2), "The Americans were guided more by broad ideological aims and short-run political considerations than by a genuine interest in the demographic substance of the conference." This politicization by the United States is ironic given that the United States was more offended than any other country at the Bucharest conference by the ideological push of the developing country coalition.

SAFE MOTHERHOOD

The strict focus on population control as a rationale for family-planning programs had started to shift by the 1980s following pressure from numerous women's rights groups, multilateral agencies, and NGOs. Objections to the coercive nature of family-planning programs in some poorer countries as well as the neglect of women's health needs contributed to changes in the political environment around population control and family planning. These changes led in 1987 to a conference sponsored by the United Nations on maternal mortality in Nairobi, Kenya, which resulted in the launch of the Safe Motherhood Initiative. The initiative raised awareness of the growing problem of maternal mortality and pushed donors to direct more resources toward maternal and child health (MCH). Organizations including the World Bank, IPPF, the Population Council, and several UN agencies subsequently formed an interagency working group that focused on making maternal health a stronger priority among international agencies and donor organizations.

The founding members of the initiative argued that global funding for family planning had concentrated too narrowly on population control while neglecting maternal mortality and morbidity in poor countries. They also contended that maternal health was often overshadowed by child survival and health, a point made in an influential scholarly article that asked, "Where is the M in MCH?" (Rosenfield and Maine, 1985). For maternal mortality rates to fall, safe motherhood could not be seen simply as a byproduct of efforts to promote the survival and health of children. Moreover, technical "magic bullets" such as the modern contraceptive methods that were the centerpiece of most family-planning programs would not be enough to reduce maternal mortality (Storeng and Béhague, 2014). For pregnancy-related deaths and complications to decline, stronger action needed to be taken to improve women's status and rectify the social and economic inequities underlying high rates of maternal mortality. Subsequent actions by other groups, such as the May 28 Day of Action organized by the Latin American & Caribbean Health Network, helped bring this message home to policymakers and advocates. By the early 1990s, NGOs across developing countries were implementing safe motherhood principles in their education campaigns and adding better maternal health programs to their health service delivery (AbouZahr, 2003).

Maternal health thus became a higher-priority target among governments and donors as the imperative of population control began to wane. The Safe Motherhood Initiative gained support by characterizing motherhood as a selfless and laudable act and emphasizing the vulnerabilities that pregnant women and mothers experience (Suh, 2017). The introduction of the Safe Motherhood Initiative coincided with the growing influence of antiabortion groups in the United States, and the initiative's emphasis on the bonds between healthy mothers and babies helped the initiative gain clout in this changing political environment. In fact, the term "safe motherhood" was specifically chosen not only to direct attention to the risks associated with pregnancy and childbirth, but also because it was an uncontroversial term that would avoid alienating conservative governments and donors (Storeng and Béhague, 2014).

The interaction between the agendas of antiabortion groups and safe motherhood proponents became complicated once safe motherhood was folded into the broader context of women's reproductive health starting in 1994. Women's rights groups and health advocates had been arguing that strengthening women's maternal health and providing women with access to reproductive health services should include the provision of safe abortions. When women's reproductive health was brought to the forefront with several major world conferences, some donors and governments who opposed abortion on moral or legal grounds had more trouble supporting maternal health programs if the programs included safe abortion services. Overall though, a growing consensus emerged at this time that maternal health is a human right, women require care during pregnancy and childbirth, maternal death is a social injustice, and governments are obligated to use their legal and health systems to reduce the risks that women face in pregnancy and childbirth (AbouZahr, 2003).

WOMEN'S REPRODUCTIVE HEALTH

Global reproductive governance underwent a third paradigm shift in 1994 with the United Nation's International Conference on Population and Development (ICPD) in Cairo, which marked a major turning point in the objectives of family-planning programs. Following widespread recognition of the failure of the Malthusian disaster predictions, the rationale for family-planning programs shifted away from simply controlling population toward promoting women's reproductive health. Feminists, women's rights groups, and other grassroots organizations had become increasingly critical of the demographic rationale behind family-planning programs. They started to organize and express stronger support for a broader range of political, social, and economic rights for women in order to address the serious health concerns that women faced. At the conference, it appeared that there was finally convergence between the voices that had pushed for family planning in order to control women's fertility, and the voices that had argued for the protection of women's reproductive rights and improvements in their economic and social status (Smyth, 1996).

Representatives at the ICPD in Cairo discussed more progressive, gender-sensitive ideas about the interactions between development, population, and individual well-being. A total of 179 countries agreed to a 20-year "Programme of Action" intended to be a thorough guide to achieving shared growth and more equitable development. This Programme of Action was viewed as groundbreaking in its formal recognition that population and development programs should be built on women's reproductive health, women's rights, and gender equality. Moreover, it emphasized the reproductive and sexual health and rights of all women, not just mothers. The conference decided on a set of targets for various program activities to achieve these broad objectives, and the United Nations Population Fund was charged with monitoring progress toward these targets.

The Cairo conference formally established the imperative to empower women in exercising their reproductive rights and the need to improve women's access to reproductive healthcare services. It was also the first official venue that recognized the importance of women's sexual rights and sexual health. Sexual rights include women's right to say no to forced, unwanted, and unprotected sex, and sexual health encompasses emotional well-being and personal relations. These definitions represent a broader application of sexual health compared to an earlier focus on family planning on sexually transmitted diseases, fertility, and counseling (Crossette, 2005; Glasier, Gülmezoglu, Schmid, Moreno, and Van Look, 2006). The objectives from the Cairo conference were reinforced by the platform for action from the Fourth World Conference for Women held just a year later in Beijing. NGOs around the globe started to respond by placing more emphasis on women's reproductive and sexual health in their healthcare services. They also become more rights-oriented and recognized the importance of women's physical and emotional well-being. Some advocates even argued that population control policies might be unnecessary if women were to gain true freedom to exercise their fundamental economic rights, have political and social agency, and employ reproductive choice (Dixon-Mueller, 1993).

While some viewed the new focus on women's reproductive health as a victory for feminists and women's rights groups in the global governance of women's fertility, critics cautioned that the paradigm shift did little to remove the structures of constraint inherent in the economies of developing countries that limited women's reproductive rights. They pointed to the work of feminist economists who argued that because the macroeconomy determines the availability of jobs and the sharing of household work burdens, it influences the distribution of income and acts as a structure of constraint on the achievement of gender equality (Elson and Çağatay, 2000). Gender inequality, in turn, limits women's expressions of agency in terms of their ability to make reproductive choices, exercise control over resources, and have mobility outside of the house. This argument has subsequently been supported with an empirical analysis showing that women's economic opportunities have a positive and statistically significant relationship with their sexual autonomy—measured by their ability to negotiate condom use (Hanmer and Klugman, 2016). Hence, macroeconomic policy reforms that ended fiscal austerity would have been crucial to supporting the Cairo agenda. These reforms would facilitate public investment in physical and social infrastructure as a means toward reducing women's unpaid care burdens and supporting their ability to obtain well-paid jobs.

The 1994 ICPD was the first global forum to institutionalize the goal of universal access to reproductive health. However, this goal was absent from an important set of development objectives formulated at the UN's Millennium Summit in 2000. A year later, when the UN formally launched the Millennial Development Goals (MDGs)—a blueprint for global development to be achieved by 2015—universal access to reproductive health was excluded from the key goals. The MDGs had eight separate goals, each with specific targets and indicators, and two of the eight goals pertained specifically to women: MDG3 aimed to achieve gender equality and empower women (with the target of eliminating gender disparity in primary and secondary education by 2005 and at all levels of education by 2015), and MDG5 aimed to improve maternal health (with the target of reducing by three-quarters the maternal mortality ratio). Conspicuously absent from these goals and targets were any references to women's reproductive and sexual health.

Although the United Nations Secretariat originally intended to have the MDGs include at least some of the language from the Cairo conference on women's reproductive and sexual rights, opposition from developing countries and lack of support from the US government prevented this from happening. In particular, the G-77, a large block of developing countries with the power to mobilize a majority vote in the UN's General Assembly, decided to act in unity against the inclusion of reproductive rights in order to avoid polarizing their more conservative members (Crossette, 2005). Even though the World Bank waged a strong campaign for the MDGs to have a clear and explicit goal on women's reproductive and sexual health, the G-77 adamantly opposed not only the inclusion of such a goal but also any relevant language embedded in one of the eight existing goals. The US government, at this time led by Democratic president Bill Clinton, did not try to intervene. Assailed from the right by conservative members of Congress and a powerful antiabortion political lobby, the Clinton administration had ceased its efforts at the UN to advocate for stronger reproductive and sexual rights for women (Crossette, 2005).

In a subsequent review of progress toward the MDGs at the World Summit in 2005, delegates formally recognized that the exclusion of reproductive health from the MDGs was a mistake and that they could not be achieved without progress in achieving universal access to women's reproductive and sexual health (Glasier et al., 2006). The summit resulted in the addition of new targets to the MDGs, including a target in MDG5 of achieving universal access to reproductive health. The specific indicators for tracking purposes included the adolescent birth rate, contraceptive prevalence, and the unmet need for contraception. In 2015, the year to which the MDGs were calibrated, many of the targets had not been reached. Thus, the UN replaced the MDGs with the Sustainable Development Goals, a set of 17 goals and 169 targets that included, from their inception, women's sexual and reproductive health and rights.

Access to safe abortions has remained largely absent from the global reproductive health agenda. However, delegates at the Cairo conference did call for the provision of postabortion care services across developing countries regardless of their national abortion legislation. Postabortion care services are designed to treat women who have complications from abortion and also provide them with birth control counseling, follow-up reproductive healthcare, and contraceptive supplies so as to break the cycle of repeated unwanted pregnancies. As a result of efforts by large NGOs such as Ipas and IPPF to prioritize postabortion care and donor funding for such services, postabortion care has become the de facto solution to the problem of unsafe abortions. Roughly 50 developing countries currently have formal programs for postabortion care (Suh, 2017).

USAID has provided financial support for postabortion care services, which are exempted from the otherwise tight restrictions imposed by the Helms Amendment on USAID involvement in abortion funding and activities. However, this support is complicated and politicized largely because MVA is used not only to perform abortions, but also in postabortion care services. Since the MVA syringe was first popularized in the early 1970s, the global health community has come to recognize MVA techniques as the safest way to complete incomplete abortions and halt bleeding following unsafe abortions (Suh, 2015). Because postabortion care is exempted from the Helms Amendment, USAID has supported MVA training for postabortion care providers. However, MVA is also used for first-trimester pregnancy terminations, so USAID could not fund MVA training for the provision of abortion services, nor could it manufacture or disseminate the technology. Moreover, USAID's support of postabortion care has been contextualized in terms of maternal health rather than women's reproductive rights (Suh, 2015). Thus, the US government, like many other donors, has not fully supported the goals set in place during the 1994 Cairo conference, especially the call for a complete spectrum of reproductive health services and a focus on all women regardless of their status as mothers.

Scholars and advocates have raised other concerns about the slow implementation of the Cairo reproductive rights agenda. They have pointed to operational and institutional impediments, including the perceived lack of urgency among policymakers and agency leaders, insufficient funding for the Programme of Action as a whole, and a general shift in priorities among some donors away from reproductive health toward HIV/AIDS programs (van Dalen and Scharf, 2103). They also raised concerns about ideologically based efforts on the part of the largest bilateral donor—the United States government under the George W. Bush administration—to refocus population assistance in a way that undermined the original reproductive health goals in the Programme of Action. These efforts included changing the content of sex education to place more emphasis on "abstinence only" curricula; postponing the introduction of over-the-counter emergency contraception; restricting access to abortion services domestically and abroad; disparaging the effectiveness and acceptability of condoms; and redirecting money away from women's reproductive health toward HIV/AIDS prevention and treatment, with much of the HIV/AIDS program hampered by an array of restrictions as well as requirements to focus on abstinence programs (Kulczycki, 2007).[6] Critics have pointed to these actions, especially those to restrict women's access to abortion, as evidence of the US government's continued attempts to regulate women's reproductive freedom in the developing world. In this sense, US policy has returned to the population control mentality of earlier decades, when controlling women's reproduction and health was a central concern of development policy and foreign aid (Murphy, 2012).

FINANCIAL ASSISTANCE FOR FAMILY PLANNING AND REPRODUCTIVE HEALTH

Financial assistance for family-planning and reproductive health services constitutes a portion of a larger category of foreign aid commonly referred to as population assistance. Since the 1994 population conference in Cairo, the United Nations Population Fund has been charged with monitoring and reporting on global resource flows for population assistance according to targets in a "costed population package." Figure 3.1 presents a summary of the global resource flows for population assistance from 1995 to 2012, the most recent year of available data. The final expenditures for the costed population package are grouped into four categories that were agreed upon at the Cairo conference: family-planning services, basic reproductive health services, STD/HIV/AIDS activities, and basic research and policy analysis (UNFPA, 2017).[7] Several noteworthy patterns emerge. First, final donor expenditures for population assistance remained fairly stagnant at or below $2 billion until 2001, after which funds climbed rapidly and steadily to $12.4 billion in 2012. Second, most of this growth was driven by increased assistance for the prevention and treatment of sexually transmitted diseases and HIV/AIDS. In fact, in 1995, assistance for STD/HIV/AIDS activities constituted just 9% of total population assistance, and 12 years later this share peaked at 75% before settling at 65% in 2012. Third, assistance for family-planning programs took the opposite course, comprising over half of all population assistance in 1995 before dropping quickly to 9% or less in every year since 2004.

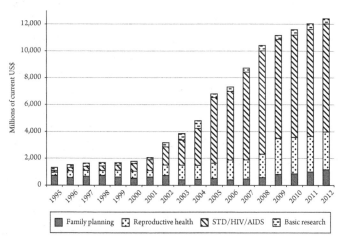

Figure 3.1 Final Donor Expenditures for Population Assistance by Program Area

Source: Constructed with data in UNFPA (2017).

Total population assistance for developing countries originates primarily from governments in high-income countries, and a small portion comes from foundations, NGOs, and development banks. As shown in Panel A of Figure 3.2, as of 2012, 90% of primary funds for population assistance came from developed countries in the form of grants, while just 5% came from grants from foundations and NGOs.[8] The remainder came from the UN and from development banks in the form of loans and grants. This allocation has changed somewhat since 1995, when bank loans were proportionately larger and the share coming from country donors was smaller. As shown in Panel B, in 2012 among the individual country donors, the United States accounted for 57% of all primary funds for population assistance, followed by the United Kingdom (10%) and the Netherlands, Germany, and Sweden (each at 4%). These proportions have not changed very much since 1995 (the earliest year of data available from the UNFPA), indicating that among all bilateral donors, the United States has remained the largest provider of population assistance. Sub-Saharan Africa is by far the largest developing region to receive primary funds for population assistance, receiving almost three-quarters of total population assistance in 2012. Interestingly, the largest foundation to provide primary funds is the Bill and Melinda Gates Foundation, donating almost 90% of all primary funds originating from foundations. Similarly, the largest NGO to provide primary funds is DKT International (92% of all funds from NGOs).[9] While NGOs operate mostly as intermediaries that channel funds from primary donors to recipient countries, some NGOs do spend their own resources on population assistance (UNFPA, 2017).

Developing countries also spend their own resources on population and development activities; in 2012 alone, developing countries spent $55.5 billion dollars on population and development goals (UNFPA, 2017). Almost 35% of that amount came from government sources, less than 1% came from local NGOs, and about 65% came from consumers as out-of-pocket expenditures. The UNFPA notes that the total amount of domestic resources, while larger than foreign assistance inflows, may be a misleading indicator of the extent to which most countries are able to finance their population and developing goals because most of these domestic resource flows come from a few large countries. Meanwhile,

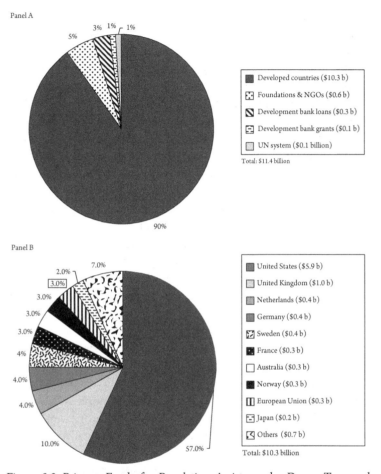

Panel A

3% 1% 1%
5%

Developed countries ($10.3 b)
Foundations & NGOs ($0.6 b)
Development bank loans ($0.3 b)
Development bank grants ($0.1 b)
UN system ($0.1 billion)

Total: $11.4 billion

90%

Panel B

7.0%
2.0%
3.0%
3.0%
3.0%
3.0%
4%
4.0%
4.0%
10.0%
57.0%

United States ($5.9 b)
United Kingdom ($1.0 b)
Netherlands ($0.4 b)
Germany ($0.4 b)
Sweden ($0.4 b)
France ($0.3 b)
Australia ($0.3 b)
Norway ($0.3 b)
European Union ($0.3 b)
Japan ($0.2 b)
Others ($0.7 b)

Total: $10.3 billion

Figure 3.2 Primary Funds for Population Assistance by Donor Type and
Source Country, 2012
Panel A: Primary Funds by Donor Type
Panel B: Primary Funds by Source Country
Source: Constructed with data in UNFPA (2017).

many countries, especially the least developed, cannot finance their own population programs and thus depend on international donors to do so.

To what extent do developing countries depend on foreign assistance to finance their population activities? In the case of contraceptives, 80% of contraceptive supplies (birth control pills, intrauterine devices, injectables, implants, and condoms) in sub-Saharan Africa are supplied by foreign donors (Ross, Weissman, and Stover, 2009). This share is much higher than in any other developing region. In Latin America and the Caribbean, about one-third of contraceptive supplies are provided by foreign donors; in the Middle East, North Africa, Asia, and the Central Asian Republics, 20% to 25% of total contraceptive supplies are funded by donors. Outside of sub-Saharan Africa, a higher proportion of contraceptives is supplied either by private-sector entities (with consumers paying out of pocket or through some mix of private-public funding) or by government agencies (funded by public-sector budgets). Despite the growth of both international assistance and domestic resources, overall there is still a substantial donor gap of about $1.4 billion for the 2008–2020 period across developing regions (Ross et al., 2009). Accounting for most of this gap is the growth in modern contraceptive users and the increased demand for condoms for HIV/AIDS prevention.

The main objectives of family-planning assistance continue to revolve around filling the unmet need for modern contraceptives and reducing unintended pregnancies. Unintended pregnancies can of course result from unprotected sex as well as contraceptive failure. How effective are the various methods of fertility control? Table 3.1, which reports contraceptive failure rates by type of method, indicates that in the first year of use, the two main traditional methods (withdrawal and periodic abstinence) fail to prevent pregnancy 13 to 14 times for every 100 instances in which they are used. At the other extreme, long-acting contraceptive methods have the lowest failure rates: implants and intrauterine devices have 0.6 and 1.4 failures per 100 instances of use, respectively. These differentials and the risk of failure increase over time. Within three years, traditional methods will result in failure about 32 to 36 times per 100 instances of use, compared to 1 to 2 failures for implants and intrauterine devices. Results for different demographic groups also indicate that failure rates

Table 3.1 RATES OF CONTRACEPTIVE FAILURE BY TYPE OF METHOD
ACROSS DEVELOPING COUNTRIES

	Median failure rate during first		
Method	12 months of use	24 months of use	36 months of use
Implants	0.6	1.0	1.1
Intrauterine device	1.4	1.9	2.1
Injectables	1.7	3.6	5.5
Pill	5.5	10.8	15.1
Male condom	5.4	13.3	16.0
Withdrawal	13.4	27.4	35.7
Periodic abstinence	13.9	25.8	32.4

Note: Median failure rate is the number of failures per 100 instances of use, based on a sample of 43 countries using the most recent year of Demographic and Health Survey data available from 1990 to 2013.
Source: Polis et al. (2016).

tend to be higher for women under the age of 25. Note that these failure rates are calculated using women's self-reports in household survey data for 43 developing countries, so they reflect typical-use failure rates in regular conditions rather than clinical failure rates in perfect conditions (Polis et al., 2016). Thus, typical-use failure rates incorporate improper use of a particular method, while clinical failure rates assume that users follow the instructions perfectly every time.

High failure rates for a particular method of fertility control become problematic when many women are using that particular method. In other words, the greater the share of women in a country using a less effective method, the higher the aggregate risk of unintended pregnancy becomes in that country. Figure 3.3 shows that among the seven regions examined in Polis et al. (2016), North Africa / West Asia stands out as the region

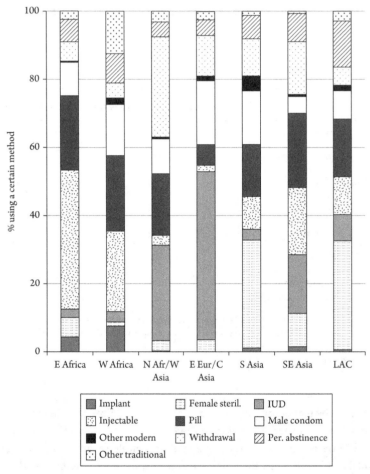

Figure 3.3 Method Mix Among Women of Reproductive Age Controlling Their Fertility
Source: Constructed with data in Polis et al. (2016).

where women have the greatest risk of experiencing an unintended pregnancy: this region has the highest prevalence of traditional methods that entail the greatest risk of contraceptive failure. In this region, 37% of women of reproductive age who are controlling their fertility report that they are using either withdrawal, periodic abstinence, or an alternative traditional method such as lactational amenorrhea. Not far behind are countries in West Africa, where on average one-quarter of women report using traditional methods.

Figure 3.3 also shows that injectables are used more intensively in East and West Africa than in any other region. In contrast, half of all women controlling their fertility in Eastern Europe and Central Asia use intrauterine devices, while female sterilization is more common in South Asia and in Latin America and the Caribbean (about one-third of women in these regions). Among the seven regions, the method mix is most balanced and diverse in Southeast Asia. Despite having higher failure rates among modern contraceptives, male condoms remain widely used across developing regions largely because they are relatively cheap and accessible. On average, 12% of all women across developing regions report that they control their fertility with condoms, with higher rates in Eastern Europe and Central Asia (19% of women) and lower rates in Southeast Asia (5%). These findings on failure rates and method mix have important implications for family-planning programs in terms the types of contraceptive methods that are made available as well as education about proper usage. Increasing the availability of a wider range of contraceptive options, including long-acting methods, constitutes an important step in empowering women and couples to select the method they are confident using and will use correctly. Providing clear information, counseling services, and follow-up care, especially for younger women, should help to improve the efficacy of family-planning programs in reducing unintended pregnancies.

DOES FAMILY PLANNING STILL MATTER?

Family planning no longer attracts the same kind of attention and funding among donors and agencies that it had previously. Global assistance for family planning has stagnated since the mid-1990s, comprising a shrinking proportion of total population assistance. Moreover, the US share among all bilateral aid donors has also leveled off. In contrast, global funding and promotion of HIV/AIDS prevention and treatment has taken off in terms of the absolute amount and relative importance in total population assistance flows. The distribution of aid, which does not align with the priorities set in place at the 1994 Cairo conference, begs the question of whether family-planning assistance still matters and, if so, why. Advocates argue that family planning should remain integrated into donor efforts to promote well-being in developing countries, while critics question the overall efficacy of foreign aid.

In a much-cited article in support of family-planning efforts, Cleland et al. (2006) argue that assessments of family-planning programs have generally found positive associations with lower fertility and population stabilization in much of Asia and Latin America. However, there is still a high unmet need for family planning in very poor countries, especially in sub-Saharan Africa. Unlike other health interventions, family-planning programs have multiple potential benefits, including lower poverty rates, reductions in maternal and infant mortality, improved agency for women to exercise reproductive choice, less strain on the environment, and higher educational attainment for girls. For these benefits to be realized, donors and agencies need to revive their advocacy and financial support for family planning in the poorest countries of the world, especially in sub-Saharan Africa. Cleland et al. (2006) argue that high fertility and population growth actually constitute a larger threat to sustainable development in these countries than the HIV/AIDS epidemic, and that the family-planning agenda need not contradict with efforts to strengthen women's reproductive and sexual rights.

Skeptics, however, question the effectiveness of foreign aid and argue it may even have detrimental impacts. Dambisa Moyo, one of the most outspoken critics of foreign aid, argues that it is often squandered through corruption and breeds aid dependency, especially in Africa (Moyo, 2009). Further criticisms of foreign aid revolve around the lack of accountability to stakeholders, the focus on grandiose plans, and the inability of foreign aid to stimulate economic growth (Easterly, 2006). Easterly compares foreign aid to central planning with external financial assistance; just as central planning cannot effectively solve economic problems and create growth, foreign aid cannot fix the problems that cause countries to remain poor. Thus, it cannot generate economic growth. Evaluations of foreign aid are more positive when it has a more specialized purpose with a specific objective, such as eradicating river blindness, providing nutritional supplements, controlling the spread of malaria with bed nets and indoor spraying, preventing HIV transmission, and providing sexual health services. The key to success in these programs is that they have focus, good transparency, accountability, and large benefits for the poor relative to the costs (Easterly and Williamson, 2011). A similar lesson applies to the work and funding of NGOs. NGOs with lofty goals rarely achieve them, while NGOs are more successful if they decide which particular projects are most effective (such as treating sexually transmitted infections and providing antiretroviral drugs) and then sustain these projects by paying local workers to implement them in ways that are consistent with the needs of the community (Swidler and Watkins, 2009). These are important lessons for improving donor initiatives to fund family-planning programs.

In 2012 the UK government and the Bill and Melinda Gates Foundation organized a large conference called the London Summit on Family Planning, which many observers interpreted as an indication that family planning has not gone out of vogue. Prompted by the waning global interest in family planning in the face of large pockets of unmet need, the organizers used the summit as an opportunity to launch a campaign called the Family Planning 2020 (FP2020) partnership. Members of the partnership made a commitment to provide an additional 120 million women with access to contraception and family-planning services in the world's 69 poorest countries by the year 2020. Estimates in Alkema, Kantorova, Menozzi, and Biddlecom (2013) indicate that the number of women with unmet need for contraception in the 69 poorest countries had risen from 99 million in 1990 to 145 million at the time of the summit. The authors projected that in the absence of the campaign, unmet need would continue to rise to 161 million women.

To date it is not clear the extent to which the FP2020 partnership has prompted a revitalization of family-planning programs. In 2017, an additional 38.8 million women and girls in the 69 poorest countries were using modern contraceptives relative to the launch of the family-planning campaign in 2012. Although this increase was approximately 30% above the historical trend, it still fell substantially below the target for new contraceptive users (FP2020 Partnership, 2017). Bilateral assistance from donor governments for family planning did increase initially after the

London summit but by 2016 had dropped back down to 2013 levels in real terms (Lief, Wexler, and Kates, 2017). It did not bode well for the FP2020 campaign that funding from the two largest donor countries fell in 2016: the United States and the United Kingdom. The declining support from the US government may even turn into substantial cutbacks under the expanded gag rule imposed by the Trump administration in 2017.

NOTES

1. For excellent reviews and comprehensive historical accounts see Petchesky (1990), Birdsall, Kelley, and Sinding (2001), Lam (2011), and Bongaarts, Cleland, Townsend, Bertrand, and Das Gupta (2012).
2. Undaunted by Eisenhower's rejection, Draper went on to play a crucial role in building the "financial architecture" around the family-planning movement (Sinding, 2007). During the 1960s he was the key person to convince Congress to allocate money in the foreign aid budget for population assistance, and he lobbied governments of other industrial countries to support the IPPF. He also helped to establish the Population Crisis Committee (which subsequently became Population Action International) and the United Nations Population Fund.
3. Although technically the Comstock Law is still on the books today, the interpretation of what is considered obscene has continued to change over time, and the Supreme Court struck down the last of the state bans on contraception in 1972.
4. Ravenholt's controversial approach caused him to make enemies both on the left (from feminists who argued that he effectively used large developing-country populations as experimental subjects of relatively untested birth control methods) and the right (from members of the Catholic Church who opposed his push for large-scale dissemination of contraceptive methods and abortion devices) (Goldberg, 2009).
5. Leading this research effort was another controversial scientist named Harvey Karman who had a history of performing illegal abortions. In 1955, one woman who sought his help died from infection, causing Karman to serve a two-year prison term. Upon his release he promptly continued with his efforts to improve abortion technology (Goldberg, 2009).
6. Another ironic twist in this historical narrative is that one of Bush's top officials to implement this agenda—the USAID Administrator and Director of U.S. Foreign Assistance—resigned following a sex scandal in which multiple media sources linked him to an escort service.

7. Final expenditures are funds that have been received by developing countries directly from donor governments or through intermediate donors; they exclude loans from development banks. Note also that data before 1999 for HIV/AIDS activities include only HIV/AIDS prevention, not treatment.

8. The UNFPA distinguishes between final expenditures (the funds received by developing countries in a given year) and primary funds (the money that originates from the primary donors in a given year). The total amounts for these two categories differ somewhat each year.

9. DKT International is a charitable non-profit organization based in the U.S. that uses social marketing techniques to promote family planning and HIV/AIDS prevention. Most of their revenue comes from the sale of low-cost contraceptives, and they are one of the world's largest private providers of family-planning products and services (DKT International, 2017). The founder, Phil Harvey, has gained international notoriety for using profits from his adults-only mail order company to help finance DKT's activities, and for standing up for free speech after refusing to sign a pledge to oppose commercial sex work (Cheshes, 2002; ACLU, 2006).

Chapter 4

Fertility and Contraceptive Use

Family-planning programs have become integral components of development strategies around the world. This emphasis is reflected by the prominence of family planning in the funding and policymaking efforts of governments, multilateral agencies, and international donors. As the previous chapter made clear, the attention to family planning is extensive, and it is not new. The US government has helped to finance family-planning programs in developing countries since the mid-1960s, and large funders such as the Bill and Melinda Gates Foundation have supported major initiatives in family planning and reproductive health. In 2005 the United Nations added universal access to reproductive health as a key target in the Millennium Development Goals. However, despite all this interest, there is still no consensus about how exactly family-planning programs affect women's unplanned pregnancies, abortion rates, and fertility.

As long as the US government has supported family-planning programs in developing countries, researchers have debated the effectiveness of such programs in managing women's fertility. In some instances fertility rates have not changed very much following increased availability of low-cost contraception through family-planning programs, while in many cases they have. How contraceptive prices and availability impact women's fertility is a surprisingly complex and controversial issue, in terms of both theory and supporting evidence. Scholars have spent decades debating whether women's fertility has responded more to changes in couples' demand for children or to changes in the availability of low-cost contraceptive methods. Some scholars have argued that changes in women's fertility outcomes arise mostly due to changes in couples' preferences for how many children to have, which in turn are affected mostly by broad changes associated with economic development. Others have developed models and have found evidence showing that fertility can be quite responsive to the supply of modern birth control methods. Intertwined in these debates is the issue of abortion and how abortion rates change when modern contraception becomes more or less accessible.

The purpose of this chapter is to present a comprehensive examination of women's decision-making around contraceptive use and fertility. This discussion will help the reader to better understand how US funding cuts for international family-planning services potentially affect women's fertility and abortion rates abroad. The chapter first offers some descriptive evidence on modern contraceptive usage and fertility rates over time and around the world. It then explores the debate over fertility and contraception using both a conceptual framework of women's fertility and a review of the empirical evidence. The framework is based on economic tools that model women's preferences and behaviors concerning fertility, and it generates a number of scenarios showing how changes in the cost of modern contraceptive methods can impact pregnancy, abortion, and fertility. The chapter also explores existing empirical evidence on the trade-off between abortion and access to contraceptives. The weight of the existing evidence supports the theoretical prediction that reductions in financial assistance for family planning are likely to have detrimental effects, including more unintended pregnancies and more, not fewer, abortions.

GLOBAL PATTERNS

Although people have had access to modern methods of birth control for about half a century, many countries still have high rates of fertility and a high unmet need for contraception. Figure 4.1 indicates the need for modern contraceptive methods and the extent to which this need has been met over time. Constructed with data from the Estimates and Projections of Family Planning Indicators Database of the United Nations Department of Economic and Social Affairs (UNDESA, 2017), this figure shows total demand, usage, and unmet need for modern contraceptive methods among married and in-union women of reproductive age for six

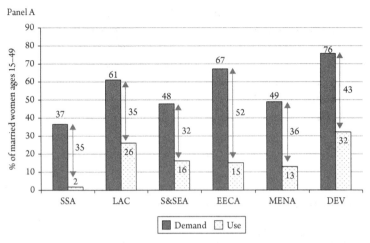

Panel A

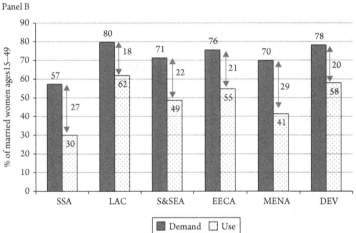

Panel B

Figure 4.1 Modern Contraceptive Demand, Use, and Unmet Need, 1970–2016
Panel A: Unmet Need (Gap between Demand and Use) in 1970
Panel B: Unmet Need (Gap between Demand and Use) in 2016
Note: SSA is sub-Saharan Africa, LAC is Latin America and the Caribbean, S&SEA is South and Southeast Asia, EECA is Eastern Europe and Central Asia, MENA is Middle East and North Africa, and DEV is developed countries. The means are unweighted.
Source: Constructed from data in UNDESA (2017) using the format in Bongaarts (2014).

geographical regions.[1] Note that by definition, having a demand for contraception is when women of reproductive age are fecund (that is, they are capable of becoming pregnant and giving birth) but do not want to become pregnant. Also, women who are currently using modern contraceptives are assumed to be meeting their demand for contraception, even if they are not satisfied with the method they are using. One can specify the relationship between these indicators as follows:

$$total\ demand = contraceptive\ use + unmet\ need.$$

As shown in Figure 4.1, in 1970 (the earliest year for which UNDESA provides data), sub-Saharan Africa had by far the lowest total demand for contraception among all regions. Just 37% of married women of reproductive age had demand for contraception, and only 2% of women were using modern contraception, leaving an unmet need of 35% of women. These numbers had improved substantially by 2016, but sub-Saharan Africa still had the lowest total demand for contraception among all regions (57%). At the opposite extreme, the Developed Countries group had considerably higher total demand for contraception than other regions in 1970. Three-quarters of women of reproductive age did not want to become pregnant, and about two-thirds of women were using modern contraception. This contraceptive usage rate was the highest among all regions. By 2016, the Developed Countries group had reduced unmet need from 43% to 20% of all women of reproductive age, but this group of countries no longer had the highest demand for and usage of modern contraceptives. With 80% of women in Latin America and the Caribbean demanding contraception and 62% of women using modern contraception, this region on average had even greater contraceptive prevalence and lower unmet need. Pushing the average prevalence rate down for the Developed Countries group are several nations in the Southern Europe subregion, including Bosnia and Herzegovina, Macedonia, Montenegro, and Serbia, which all have very low contraceptive usage and fairly high unmet need.

Interestingly, in 1970 every region in the figure had substantial unmet need for modern contraception, ranging from 32% of women in South and Southeast Asia, to 52% in Eastern Europe and Central Asia. Ironically, sub-Saharan Africa was actually at the lower end of this range of estimates for unmet need, and the Developed Countries group was at the higher end. By 2016, unmet need had fallen in all regions, especially in Eastern Europe and Central Asia. Lagging the most has been the Middle East and North Africa region, which by 2016 showed the least improvement in reducing unmet need, and this region still had the largest absolute gap between contraceptive demand and use. Sub-Saharan Africa also lagged in terms of closing the gap between demand and use. Not only is contraceptive availability a problem, but women in a number of these countries still face stigmas associated with using modern contraceptive methods.

Similar points can be made when looking at how modern contraceptive demand, use, and unmet need relate to real GDP per capita for individual countries. This information is provided in Figure 4.2, where three separate panels provide scatterplot diagrams of the respective measure of contraception against real GDP per capita in US$ adjusted for cost of living (World Bank, 2017). All data are for the year 2016. Superimposed on each scatterplot is a curve to approximate the relationship between each measure of contraception and real GDP per capita. This curve is derived from a locally weighted scatterplot-smoothing technique that creates a smooth line through a scatterplot to help visualize the relationship between variables. Also by way of explanation, each country is assigned one of six markers according to its relevant geographical region.

The first panel of Figure 4.2 shows that contraceptive demand rises rapidly as we move from very low-income countries (generally in sub-Saharan Africa) to higher-income developing countries (generally in South and Southeast Asia and in Latin America and the Caribbean). At approximately a level of $20,000 in real GDP per capita, the smoothed curve tapers off and stays roughly constant. The dip down at the high end of the income distribution reflects the relatively low contraceptive demand in several very high-income countries—Qatar, Kuwait, United Arab Emirates, and Singapore. A similar pattern is seen in the second panel, which shows the percentage of married and in-union women of reproductive age who are using modern contraceptives. In particular, usage rates increase rapidly for countries moving from very low real GDP per capita to levels of about $20,000, and then the usage rates increase very slowly before tapering off again for the wealthiest nations, which are predominantly in the Middle East.

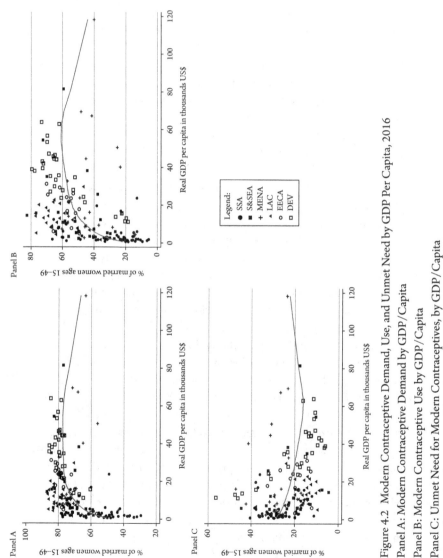

Figure 4.2 Modern Contraceptive Demand, Use, and Unmet Need by GDP Per Capita, 2016

Panel A: Modern Contraceptive Demand by GDP/Capita

Panel B: Modern Contraceptive Use by GDP/Capita

Panel C: Unmet Need for Modern Contraceptives, by GDP/Capita

As shown in Figure 4.2, a handful of developed countries (mostly in Southern Europe) have low income and very low usage of modern contraception. On the flip side, there are a number of relatively poor countries that have extremely high prevalence of modern contraception, quite a bit higher than many wealthy countries. These high-use countries include Brazil, China, Costa Rica, Nicaragua, and Thailand, each of which has contraceptive usage rates that exceed 75%. The third panel of Figure 4.2 shows the expected downward-sloping curve for unmet need for modern contraceptives as countries become richer. The curve gradually declines until real GDP per capita reaches a level of about $60,000, and then the curve rises slightly for a few outlying countries (mostly rich nations in the Middle East) with high unmet need for modern contraception.

The remaining two figures in this section on global patterns illustrate total fertility rates over time and across countries and regions. The total fertility rate is defined to be the total number of children born or likely to be born to a woman over her lifetime if she were to experience the prevailing age-specific fertility rates in the population through her lifetime. It is a projected rate rather than the actual number of children born to a woman over her lifetime. A total fertility rate of about 2.1 children per woman is generally considered to be replacement-level fertility. Data on total fertility rates were obtained from UNDESA's (2015a) database World Fertility Data 2015, the most up-to-date database available on fertility rates around the globe. Consistent with the data on contraceptive use, there are data for 185 countries. Data were extracted for the 1970 to 2014 period, with 2014 being the most recent year available. Note that most countries had missing values in at least some of the years during this period.[2]

Figure 4.3 compares the average total fertility rate across the six geographical regions in 1990 and 2010, two years in which most countries had observed values for the total fertility rate. One can see that sub-Saharan Africa had considerably higher total fertility rates (6.2 and 5.0 children per woman) in both years relative to the other regions. Closely related, the absolute decrease in fertility was not as great in sub-Saharan Africa as it was in other regions, especially in the Middle East and North Africa, where the average fertility rate fell by almost two births, from 4.4 to 2.7 children per woman. South and Southeast Asia also saw a large decline in total

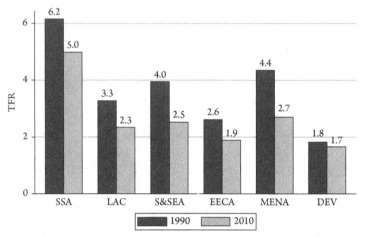

Figure 4.3 Total Fertility Rates by Geographical Region, 1990–2010
Note: Regional means are unweighted.
Source: Constructed from data in UNDESA (2017).

fertility, from 4.0 to 2.5 children per woman. Because developed countries as a whole have already undergone their demographic transitions, total fertility fell just slightly, from 1.8 to 1.7 children per woman, below the replacement rate.

The final figure in this section (Figure 4.4) illustrates the relationship between country-level fertility rates and contraceptive demand, contraceptive use, and unmet need. Note that each panel shows 185 datapoints representing the total fertility rate and contraceptive indicator for each country in the most recent year for which there was an observed value for total fertility (on average, this year was 2011). As before, superimposed on each scatterplot is a curve that approximates the association between total fertility and each contraceptive measure using the same locally weighted scatterplot-smoothing technique. Panel A clearly shows that as the demand for modern contraceptives rises, the total fertility rate falls. Most countries with very low contraceptive demand and high fertility are in sub-Saharan Africa, while most countries with very high contraceptive demand and low fertility are in the Developed Countries group and in South and Southeast Asia. Panel B shows a similar relationship between total

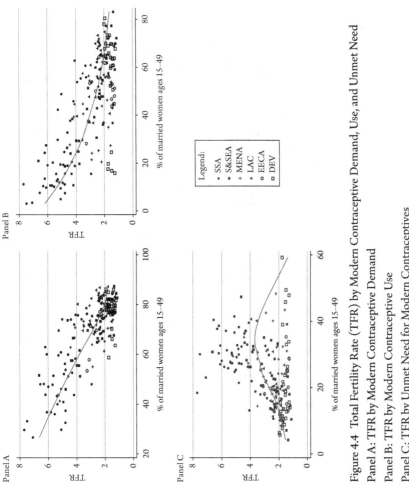

Figure 4.4 Total Fertility Rate (TFR) by Modern Contraceptive Demand, Use, and Unmet Need
Panel A: TFR by Modern Contraceptive Demand
Panel B: TFR by Modern Contraceptive Use
Panel C: TFR by Unmet Need for Modern Contraceptives

fertility rates and modern contraceptive usage. Interestingly, the curve is slightly more concave in Panel B, suggesting that the trade-off between contraceptive usage and the total fertility rate happens more quickly as women first begin to use more modern contraceptives, and then the trade-off levels off somewhat.

Finally, Panel C shows that the relationship between total fertility and the unmet need for contraception is positive for most of the distribution—that is, as the unmet need for contraception increases, the total fertility rate also increases. It is the reverse direction of this association that is the main rationale for investments in family-planning programs: as the unmet need for contraception decreases, total fertility rates fall. The countries with the highest unmet need and the highest fertility tend to be in sub-Saharan Africa, and countries at the opposite end of the spectrum with low unmet need and low fertility tend to be in South and Southeast Asia and in the Developed Countries category. Note that the curve's positive slope does become negative at the upper end of the distribution, with several countries that have very high unmet need for contraception but low total fertility. These outliers are primarily in the Southern European subregion of the Developed Countries category (especially Albania, Bosnia and Herzegovina, and Macedonia), and in the Middle East and North Africa (especially Azerbaijan).

These simple correlations suggest that fertility declines in developing countries can be attributed to reductions in unmet need for contraception and a decrease in unintended pregnancies. The next section places this relationship into context with a conceptual framework for women's decision-making around fertility. A well-designed theoretical framework can help us better understand the potential impacts of investments in family-planning programs that improve the availability of low-cost contraception.

CONCEPTUAL FRAMEWORK

Economic models can help us make predictions about how a policy change will affect decision-making. In this case we are interested in the choices that women make about sexual activity, contraceptive choice, abortion, and number of children. These decisions are usually made jointly between women and their partners, but for ease of exposition this chapter will make reference to women as the primary agents in the decision-making process. Women's fertility determinants are inherently difficult to model because the decisions involve a high degree of uncertainty. Without a form of contraception that is 100% effective, sexual activity might result in pregnancy or it might not, and decisions about whether to have an abortion or give birth if pregnancy does occur also involve a complex mix of information, preferences, costs, and risks, each factor having the potential to change in unpredictable ways.

Consistent with Frank Notestein's early work on the demographic transition and Gary Becker's seminal work on women's fertility behavior, early theoretical models of women's fertility focused mostly on the demand for children, and they made very strict assumptions about risks and uncertainties associated with fertility decisions (Notestein, 1945, 1953; Becker, 1960, 1981). In these early models, any changes in fertility over time are driven by economic development and modernization. As countries develop, the cost of having children increases (both the direct cost, such as their schooling, and the opportunity cost of women's time through higher wages in the labor market). Moreover, development brings more economic opportunities as well as new sources of social security for parents, so the economic value of children falls as they are no longer needed to contribute to household income and financial security. As a result, couples desire fewer children.

An important assumption in these early models is that women have full control over their fertility at zero cost, and they know with complete certainty before they become pregnant what the total (financial, time, and emotional) costs and benefits will be of having a child. Hence, a woman can use contraception that works perfectly and is cost-free until she decides that the benefits of having a child outweigh the disadvantages and she is ready to become pregnant. Women will not become pregnant if they perceive that they will be worse off from having a child. Consequently, all pregnancies are wanted, and there is no need to have an induced abortion. These assumptions are unrealistic, but the early models of fertility did fit some broad empirical regularities, especially when it came to declining total fertility rates over time as economic development led to greater educational attainment, higher wages, and more employment opportunities, especially for women.

More recent models of fertility, motivated by Richard Easterlin's theoretical work on the economics of fertility, have relaxed these rather strong assumptions, especially by acknowledging that women cannot perfectly control their fertility and by allowing for contraception that entails costs (financial and otherwise) and risks of failure (Easterlin, 1975, 1978). Also incorporated into more recent models are women's decisions about what type of contraception to use and the level at which to use it, which Levine (2004) refers to as contraceptive intensity. Higher contraceptive intensity reduces the likelihood of pregnancy, but the highest levels of contraceptive intensity (such as complete abstinence and sterilization) also have the greatest costs. Hence, women's choices around contraceptive intensity in their sexual lives are shaped by their desire to maximize their utility, subject to the probability of becoming pregnant and the costs of using contraception. Family-planning programs fit into these models because they are designed to help women and their partners determine with fewer constraints whether to have children, when to have them, and how many to have.[3]

As an example of a more recent economic model of fertility, Figure 4.5 shows graphically the level of contraceptive intensity that a woman will choose and what happens when the price of contraception increases. Underlying the model is the idea that sexually active women who are not intending to become pregnant will increase their contraceptive intensity in order to reduce the probability of becoming pregnant. However, greater levels of contraceptive intensity involve higher costs. These costs include the monetary costs of purchasing a particular contraceptive method or undergoing a medical procedure, the time costs of traveling to a location that provides the contraceptive method, and the emotional and physical costs of using a particular method (such as the stress of negotiating with a partner or the pain of going through a procedure). Consistent with the model developed in Levine (2004), the marginal cost of using contraception is defined as $\Delta C / \Delta P$, where ΔC is the change in total cost of using a particular level of contraceptive intensity, and ΔP is the change in probability of avoiding pregnancy. Thus, if a woman wants to increase the probability of avoiding pregnancy, she needs to spend more money, time, or emotional energy on increasing her contraceptive intensity.

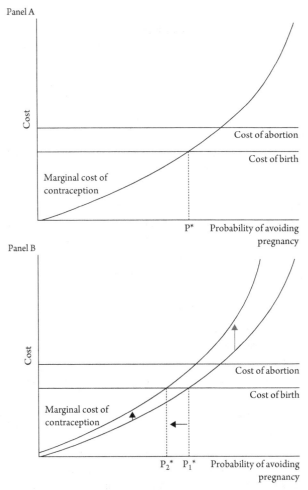

Figure 4.5 Conceptual Framework for Fertility and Contraceptive Use
Panel A: Basic Model of the Contraception Decision
Panel B: Effect of Increase in the Cost of Contraception
Source: Adapted from Levine (2004).

As shown in Panel A of Figure 4.5, the marginal cost of contraceptive intensity increases at a slightly increasing rate; that is, the marginal cost curve is slightly concave rather than straight. At what point will women choose a particular level of contraceptive intensity? This happens when the marginal cost of contraceptive intensity equals the net cost of having a child. The cost of birth is represented by a horizontal line, which implies that the cost is the same at all points of contraceptive intensity. Giving birth has various kinds of financial, temporal, emotional, and physical costs as well as various benefits; one can think of the cost of birth as the expected value of the pregnancy outcome. This model further builds in the possibility that women who are sexually active while using contraception might experience an unintended pregnancy. In this case, they need to decide whether they will have an abortion or give birth. Abortions also entail costs (financial and otherwise) that need to be incorporated into women's decision-making processes.

Panel A depicts the cost of abortion as a horizontal line, which means that the cost of abortion is constant at all points of contraceptive intensity. As before, the cost of abortion can extend beyond monetary outlays to include time and emotional costs. In the case illustrated, the cost of abortion is greater than the cost of giving birth. Women will choose the level of contraceptive intensity at which the marginal cost of contraception equals the cost of birth, resulting in a probability P^* of avoiding pregnancy. If a woman does experience contraceptive failure and becomes pregnant, she will choose to give birth. However, greater expected costs of having a child relative to the benefits will increase the chances that women will have an abortion. Similarly, if the cost of abortion is relatively low, say in a country where abortion is legally available upon request and subsidized by the public sector, it could be that the horizontal line for the cost of abortion falls below the line for the cost of birth. In this case, women will choose the level of contraceptive intensity at which the marginal cost of contraception equals the cost of abortion, and if a woman does become pregnant, she will choose to have an abortion.

Panel B of Figure 4.5 illustrates the effect of an increase in the marginal cost of using contraception, as could happen as a result of foreign aid reductions and the closure of family-planning clinics. Such closures could lead to price increases of various types of modern contraceptives due to relative scarcity, and they could also increase the time it takes for women to travel to clinics that remain open to obtain their contraceptive supplies. In the example shown, the marginal cost curve shifts up for all levels of contraceptive intensity, and it shifts up by greater amounts as the level of intensity increases. This shift in the marginal cost curve changes the point at which the marginal cost of contraception equals the cost of birth. Following the shift, a woman chooses a lower level of contraceptive intensity, and the new equilibrium probability of avoiding pregnancy shifts left from P_1^* to P_2^*. If a woman's contraception fails and she does become pregnant, she will choose to give birth.

In this case, the model predicts that the health clinic closures due to the foreign aid reduction will lead women to choose a lower level of contraceptive intensity, which is likely to increase unintended pregnancies and fertility. However, if the cost of abortion is relatively low compared to the cost of birth (so that the placement of the two horizontal lines is reversed), then the woman chooses the point at which the marginal cost of contraception equals the cost of abortion. If she does become pregnant, she will choose to have an abortion. Overall then, depending on the cost parameters, the model is consistent with an increase in unintended pregnancies, abortions, and fertility.

This model is rather simple in that the cost curves implicitly incorporate a number of factors that complicate women's decisions around contraception, abortion, and giving birth. These factors include customary beliefs, religion, philosophical views, perceptions about the comfort and safety of each method, education, employment, and any institutional restrictions that women face. Another example of an economic model of women's fertility that also incorporates some of these complications into the cost of contraception and abortion is the model developed in Jones (2015). This study uses the following production function to represent women's fertility:

$$F = f(T, M, A, \varepsilon). \tag{4.1}$$

In this equation, a woman's actual fertility depends on her use of three methods to control her fertility: traditional contraceptive methods T (such as withdrawal, lactational amenorrhea, and intermittent abstinence), modern contraceptive methods M (such as condoms, birth control pills, and intrauterine devices), and induced abortion A. The woman's actual fertility also depends on an idiosyncratic element represented by the term ε, which includes both random chance and her natural fecundity (assumed to be a given and not changeable by the woman's actions). These three methods of birth control each have an inverse relationship with women's fertility. The use of both modern contraceptives and induced abortion depends on the pecuniary and time costs of accessing them, while the traditional methods are assumed to be free and to involve no time costs. All three options also involve "utility costs," which encompass social, religious, philosophical, and institutional factors related to birth control and abortion. The key decision in this model is for a woman to choose the appropriate levels of T, M, and/or A that will prevent her actual fertility F from exceeding her desired fertility F^*, subject to the constraints she faces regarding the monetary, time, and utility costs of each method.

There are numerous examples of what the model refers to as utility costs that influence a woman's decision-making about fertility.[4] She could live in a region where people commonly believe that the birth control pill and other hormone-based contraceptives cause cancer, infertility, and other health complications. She could live in a country in which people commonly rely only on withdrawal and condoms. She might not have much agency or voice in negotiations with her intimate partner about birth control methods. She could adhere to the views of a religion such as Catholicism that condemns abortion and considers artificial birth control to be immoral. She could live in a community in which there are social stigmas associated with talking about or using particular birth control options. She might be reluctant to undergo a pelvic exam and other tests that doctors in some countries are required to perform before prescribing a contraceptive method.

She might be skeptical of getting an intrauterine device or implant if she is uncomfortable with going through the insertion procedure and leaving an object inside her body. She might not want to keep the baby if she was raped or if she got back test results indicating a severe birth defect. She might live in a country in which abortion is very common and socially accepted because historically modern methods of contraception were less available. In contrast, she could live in a country in which abortion is illegal in all cases except to save a woman's life. She might live in a country where she can buy abortion pills on the black market or through the internet. She might live in a country with a shortage of trained medical personnel and sterile facilities, making it difficult to get a safe abortion. She might have higher education and be more knowledgeable about the benefits and risks of alternative modern methods of contraception. These various scenarios are all examples of the factors that women in different countries take into account as they make choices about birth control and try to ensure that their actual fertility remains as close to their desired fertility as possible.

What might happen if the cost of using modern contraception rises? This model traces the effect of such an increase, which might feasibly arise should local healthcare providers experience funding cuts and reductions in the supply of contraceptives from foreign donors. Such reductions are likely to raise the price of contraceptives and potentially increase the time women need to find a reproductive healthcare provider. These changes are expected to impact women's contraceptive usage, abortion, and actual fertility in ways that vary by women's ability to absorb the higher costs, as well as the norms, beliefs, and institutional constraints associated with fertility control. When the price of modern contraception (M) rises, a woman will either pay the higher amount or reduce the intensity by which she uses M. If she lowers the intensity of using M, she then might increase her usage of traditional methods (T) in order to avoid exceeding her desired fertility F^*. If she becomes pregnant, she might choose abortion (A) in her attempt to maintain F^*. The extent to which she reoptimizes her decisions around T, M, and A depends not only on her ability to pay for M but also on the utility costs of these birth control methods and the form of the production function (f).

We can use the Jones (2015) model to make alternative predictions for different categories of women depending on their income level and education. First, the model predicts an increase in pregnancy for women who make the following two decisions: (1) the woman reduces the intensity of using M, and (2) the woman does not completely offset the reduced M with an increase in T. A woman will reduce her use of M if she cannot afford the monetary cost of M (because she is poor), or if she cannot afford to take the extra time to travel further away to obtain M (because she is employed). A woman will not completely offset the reduction in M with traditional methods if she has little knowledge of how to effectively use traditional methods to prevent a pregnancy or if the utility costs of using T are high. The predicted outcomes for women who do experience an unintended pregnancy are either induced abortion or giving birth. A woman will choose not to have an abortion if she cannot afford the monetary cost of an abortion or if the utility costs of having an abortion are high. The likelihood of these outcomes occurring depends on women's preferences, characteristics, and constraints. The next section examines how well the empirical evidence supports these predictions.

DEBATE ON FAMILY PLANNING AND FERTILITY OUTCOMES

Scholars have long debated the social and economic determinants of women's fertility and the importance of family-planning programs in increasing contraceptive use and reducing fertility. One group has found evidence to support what we will label the "demand for children" view. Motivated in part by Gary Becker's early theoretical work on fertility, these scholars argue that, by and large, couples succeed in having the target number of children they desire to have. Major changes in women's fertility have occurred mostly due to preferences for the ideal number of children rather than improved access to contraception through family-planning programs. Hence, countries that have seen declines in fertility have done so because women and their partners changed their preferences toward having fewer children, not because the availability of contraception has improved or its price has fallen. The major determinants of couples' desires to have fewer children are broad economic, social, and political forces associated with development. Also driving the impetus to have fewer children are the changes in women's lives that increase the opportunity cost of staying at home. Such changes would include higher educational attainment and improved labor market opportunities for women.

The other group of scholars adheres to what we will label the "unmet need" view. Prompted by models such as those developed around Figure 4.5 and Equation 4.1, scholars who support the "unmet need" view argue that countries with high fertility rates still have substantial unmet need for modern contraceptive methods, and reductions in price and improvements in the availability of contraception can cause substantial decreases in unintended pregnancies and fertility. One implication of this view is that the prevalence of contraception explains most of the variation across countries in fertility rates. Researchers adhering closely to this view acknowledge that economic development can bring about reductions in ideal family size, but it is the effort of family-planning programs to reduce the obstacles that women face in using modern contraceptive methods that is the main force behind lower fertility rates.

In practice, the evidence on access to modern contraceptives and fertility outcomes is not clear cut, with numerous rigorous studies providing support for both points of view.[5] In line with the "demand for children" view, Pritchett (1994) used data from the World Fertility Surveys and the Demographic and Health Surveys for a large sample of developing countries and found that virtually all of the differences (about 90%) across countries in actual fertility rates are explained by differences in desired fertility. Moreover, contraceptive prevalence has no statistically significant effect on excess fertility (that is, the proportion of births that are unintended) and very little effect on actual fertility after controlling for desired fertility. Pritchett acknowledged that some highly intensive and focused family-planning programs can reduce fertility rates in localized areas. However, the study maintained that on average across countries and over time, fertility responds very little to incremental changes in contraceptive availability and access to family planning.

The Pritchett study represented a fairly sweeping endorsement of the idea that broad changes associated with economic development cause women to want fewer children, while access to modern contraception has little to no effect. Other studies have also found evidence along these lines, albeit with greater nuance and more importance assigned to the role of family-planning programs. For example, Gertler and Molyneaux (1994) examined Indonesia's large fertility decline between 1982 and 1987 using econometric methods and found that detailed measures of the country's family-planning programs accounted for just 4% to 8% of the fertility decline. Most of the growing demand for contraception was caused by greater educational attainment for women and higher wages. The authors note that Indonesia already had a strong network of family-planning facilities in place during the period of analysis, implying that previous investments in family-planning infrastructure and services were important in meeting the new increased demand for contraceptive supplies.

Another example is Miller (2010), a study that evaluated how the expansion of one of the world's largest and most established family-planning programs—Colombia's Profamilia—affected fertility rates. One of the problems in accurately identifying the impact of family-planning programs on fertility is that actual contraceptive usage is determined by both the demand for contraception (which is related to women's desired fertility) and the supply of contraception (which is related to healthcare providers' available stocks). The Miller study was able to address this problem and isolate the supply effects by taking advantage of the random nature of Profamilia's expansion across Colombia's municipalities and over time since it was founded in 1965. Results indicate that even though Profamilia's expansion contributed to a postponement of the first birth and an average reduction of 0.5 births among women who had ever given birth, the program accounted for less than 10% of the overall fertility decline in areas served by the program. Miller concludes that this large-scale family-planning program played just a modest role in explaining Colombia's fertility decline, while other economic and social changes mattered more.

Siding more strongly with the "unmet need" view, a number of studies for developing countries have found evidence showing that family-planning programs do impact fertility in a meaningful way. In a direct response to the Pritchett (1994) analysis, Bongaarts (1994) countered that carefully planned programs do reduce unwanted fertility, and unwanted fertility represents a nonnegligible proportion of overall fertility in developing countries. Using what he argued was an improved methodology and a more suitable analytic sample, the author found that his measure of family-planning program effort led to a substantial decline in unwanted fertility. Moreover, Bongaarts emphasized a point trivialized by Pritchett: family-planning programs matter not only because they provide inexpensive contraceptive methods, but also because they help to empower women by making them more knowledgeable about how to use birth control and how to overcome potential stigma and disapproval from family members.

These arguments are echoed in Debpuur et al. (2002), a study evaluating a large community health and family-planning project in northern Ghana that provided extensive family-planning services, including not only contraceptive supplies but also reproductive health education and service delivery from trained nurses. The authors found that during the first three years of the program, the total fertility rate declined by one full birth, representing a 15% decline in fertility compared to communities that were not exposed to the program. A decline in fertility of similar magnitude was found for an experimental family-planning program in the Matlab district of Bangladesh (Sinha, 2005; Joshi and Schultz, 2013). Introduced in 1978, this program drastically cut the monetary, time, and utility costs of contraception by providing intensive family-planning services through regular home visits by outreach workers, dissemination of contraceptive information and supplies, and support by medical facilities in the treatment areas. Sinha's (2005) findings indicate that the average lifetime fertility of women who were exposed to the Matlab program was 0.60 births less than women who did not receive services through the program, which amounts to a 14% reduction in lifetime fertility for women in the program areas. Estimates in Joshi and Schultz (2013) are slightly larger, with a reduction of 0.78 births per woman and a 16% reduction in lifetime fertility. Overall, these estimates for Ghana and Bangladesh are large in absolute terms and relative terms compared to estimates for program effects in other countries.

This debate in the scholarly literature on the effectiveness of family-planning programs is fueled partly by the challenge of accurately identifying the program impacts on women's fertility. One challenge is isolating the program impact from other contemporaneous changes—such as changes in attitudes and social norms about the ideal family size—that could influence women's fertility decisions. Authors have tried to address this problem of endogeneity bias with econometric techniques that control for contemporaneous changes, but skeptics have still pointed to weaknesses in their identification strategies. A related issue is that family-planning programs are often started in areas where the need is greater, so the estimates of program impacts suffer from selection bias. Intuitively, this problem occurs when program placement, rather than being random, depends on program need, resulting in estimated impacts that could be biased because they reflect both the effect of the program on fertility and the effect of fertility (and its determinants) on the placement and allocation of the program. This problem is usually addressed by conducting randomized trials in the field with treatment groups that experience the program and control groups that do not. These experimental studies address the randomization problem. However, because the trials are often small-scale due to their high cost, their results are subject to the criticism of potentially not being applicable to larger populations.

Further complicating the question of program effectiveness is the fact that family-planning programs often have multiple components and objectives, including lowering the price of contraceptives, making new methods available, building the distribution infrastructure to improve contraceptive access, educating couples about birth control, and providing other healthcare services. It can be difficult to disentangle the effects of these different program components, making it harder to understand why and how family-planning programs have an effect. One study that tackled this problem is McKelvey, Thomas, and Frankenberg (2012), which looked specifically at the goal of keeping contraceptive prices low, a common component of family-planning programs across countries. The cost of service provision can be high, so it is important to know how couples respond to the availability of more affordable contraception. Using household survey data from Indonesia during the late 1990s, when Indonesia experienced a severe financial crisis, the authors found that the choices made by couples regarding whether or not to use contraception and what method to use responded very little to the large fluctuations in contraceptive prices and household income during this period. One interpretation of these small estimates of price and income responsiveness is that the heavy price subsidies for contraception built into many family-planning programs, while intended to increase contraceptive use, might in fact not be necessary.

This result is consistent with earlier findings for Indonesia by Molyneaux and Gertler (2000), which found that price subsidies for contraception between 1986 and 1994 had just a small effect on fertility (about a 3% to 6% reduction), while expansions in the distribution infrastructure and network had a considerably larger impact in reducing overall fertility. This result suggests that women had been constrained more by access and availability than they had been by price. Related to this point about different components of family-planning programs, women's preferences for the nonprice attributes of particular contraceptive methods and service delivery could matter more than price. One such attribute is the way in which family-planning service providers distribute contraception and the extent to which women can conceal their contraceptive use from their partners. As argued in Ashraf, Field, and Lee (2014), men on average have larger ideal family sizes than women, and these asymmetric preferences might lead women to conceal their contraceptive use from their partners. The authors conducted a field experiment in Zambia and found that if women could receive family-planning services alone, without their husbands present, then they were considerably more likely to seek family planning, use a concealable method of contraception (implant or injectable), and reduce their fertility. The results suggest that women's fertility might be quite responsive to how the service delivery is designed and what types of contraception are made available.

The discussion of the "demand for children" view and the "unmet need" view of contraception and women's fertility has pointed to disagreement over the extent to which family-planning programs work to reduce fertility. This disagreement stems from differences in methodology, the countries and regions subject to investigation, and the particular component of family-planning programs being analyzed. There is considerable debate over the extent to which lowering the price of contraceptives helps to reduce fertility. There seems to be less disagreement about the importance of family-planning programs in developing stronger distribution networks and infrastructure that make contraceptives more accessible. Also important is training health professionals in birth control counseling, implementing education and communication campaigns to help couples make more informed choices, and empowering women to bargain more effectively with their partners about using contraception. As argued in Bongaarts (2014), the information, education, and communication aspects of family-planning programs can work to raise the demand for contraception and lower the demand for children. These confounding effects can result in very small estimates of the effect of family-planning programs in reducing unmet needs for contraception, a complication that needs to be kept in mind when assessing the effectiveness of family-planning programs.

CONTRACEPTION AND ABORTION: COMPLEMENTS OR SUBSTITUTES?

A direct implication of the conceptual framework is that abortion rates will fall as contraceptive use increases because women are better able to meet their demand for contraception and prevent unwanted fertility. However, as we saw with the scholarship on women's fertility and family-planning programs, there is also a long-running debate on the relationship between abortion and modern contraception. In some countries, the evidence shows that abortion and modern contraceptive methods are clear substitutes, while in other countries both abortion rates and contraceptive use have risen together or declined together. Hence, even though theory predicts that they will be substitutes, it is possible for the empirics to show otherwise.

One could use a number of theoretical scenarios to predict an inverse relationship between contraception and abortion. Using the framework already developed around Figure 4.5, I argued that if abortion is relatively cheaper than the cost of birth (so that the horizontal line for the cost of abortion lies below the line for the cost of birth), then an increase in the marginal cost of contraception will prompt reduced contraceptive intensity and a lower probability of avoiding an unintended pregnancy, thus causing an increase in the likelihood of a woman seeking an abortion. The same argument could apply in the opposite direction with an increase in a woman's contraceptive intensity and a lower likelihood of needing to seek an abortion. Recall that the costs of contraception and abortion include price, availability, and social costs. A similar set of predictions arise from the framework developed with Equation 4.1. To what extent is this prediction of substitutability between contraception and abortion supported with data?

At the global level, abortion rates have declined since 1990 (Sedgh et al., 2016). Coupled with the growing prevalence of modern contraception, this pattern suggests that abortion and contraception are indeed substitutes. Declining abortion concurrent with rising contraceptive prevalence has also been demonstrated with time-series data for several specific countries (Kazakhstan, Kyrgyz Republic, Uzbekistan, Bulgaria, Turkey, Tunisia, and Switzerland) in Marston and Cleland (2003). The substitution of contraception for abortion was especially dramatic in a number of Eastern European and Central Asian countries. Abortion had constituted one of the main forms of fertility control in this region, but after the collapse of Communism and the disintegration of the Soviet Union in 1989, modern contraceptives became more accessible and abortion rates dropped sharply (Westoff, Sharmanov, Sullivan, and Croft, 1998). However, these associations are statistical correlations rather than estimates of causal effects. It could be that other broad forces such as a change in social norms caused both the increase in contraceptive use and the decline in abortions. More targeted evidence from the Matlab experiment in Bangladesh suggests that abortion rates fell in villages receiving intensive family-planning services as greater contraceptive usage led to fewer unintended pregnancies (Rahman, DaVanzo, and Razzaque, 2001). However, the Matlab family-planning program included not only the provision of low-cost contraceptives but also abortion and healthcare services, making it difficult to isolate the impact of contraceptive access on abortion rates.

More rigorous methods are needed. Miller and Valente's (2016) study of Nepal is one of surprisingly few studies to plausibly demonstrate the substitutability between contraception and abortion in a developing country.[6] The authors examined the 2004 legalization and subsequent expansion of abortion services in Nepal, a large policy change that was not accompanied by any other concurrent changes in contraceptive costs or health policy. Results indicate that each addition of a legal abortion center to a district where a woman lives is associated with a 2.6% decline in the odds of a woman using any contraceptive. Given the number of legal abortion centers that became available after legalization took place, this change amounts to a two-percentage-point decline in overall contraceptive use. Assuming that this substitutability operates in the opposite direction, the results imply that an increase in the supply of modern contraceptives can help to reduce abortions.

Other countries have seen simultaneous increases in contraceptive use and abortion rates. Two examples are Cuba and South Korea, both of which experienced increased contraceptive use and more abortions during periods of rapid fertility decline and the expansion of family-planning services (Noble and Potts, 1996). Another example is Romania, where abortion and family planning were criminalized in 1966 by dictator Nicolae Ceaușescu. Birth rates doubled the next year, largely because abortion had been the primary method of birth control before the ban. When the policy on abortions and contraception was liberalized in 1989 following the overthrow of the Communist regime, abortions and contraceptive use both rose dramatically, and the total fertility rate dropped sharply (Pop-Eleches, 2006). Marston and Cleland (2003) also found simultaneous increases in contraceptive use and abortion in four additional countries (Denmark, the Netherlands, the United States, and Singapore). The authors posit that these concurrent increases in contraception and abortion were due to dramatic declines in desired fertility and the inability of contraceptive use alone to meet women's needs for controlling fertility. Once the demographic transition slowed and fertility rates stabilized in several of the countries, abortion rates dropped while contraceptive use continued to increase, consistent with the predictions of the conceptual framework.

CONCLUSION

This chapter has examined the relationship between contraception and fertility in order to better understand how women's fertility might respond to funding cuts for family-planning programs arising from the global gag rule. Evidence from current cross-country data shows a positive relationship between unmet need for modern contraception and total fertility rates; that is, the greater the unmet need, the higher is women's fertility. This pattern is consistent with the predictions of a simple economic model of women's fertility decisions. In the model, women might experience higher pregnancy rates if the contraceptive cost increase arising from cutbacks in family-planning programs is sufficiently high to reduce their use of modern contraceptives, and if women do not fully compensate with effective use of traditional methods.

As unintended pregnancies increase, women's actual fertility might rise if abortion is not a viable alternative due to possible legal, financial, or personal constraints. The model predicts an increase in abortions for those women who become pregnant as a result of reduced access to contraceptive services, if they wish to maintain their desired fertility and do not face constraints on abortion. In this case, contraception and abortion are seen as substitutes when contraception becomes relatively expensive or difficult to obtain and abortion becomes a necessary fertility control option. These predictions are crucial for understanding why and how restrictions in US family-planning assistance have direct impacts on women's intimate lives and fertility behavior.

The chapter has also pointed to considerable debate on the extent to which these predictions hold up to empirical evidence. Some of the variation in the conclusions authors have made about the effectiveness of family-planning programs comes from differences in the methodologies and sample countries. On balance, while there is less agreement on the extent to which women's fertility responds to changes in the price of contraception, there appears to be greater consensus that other components of family-planning programs besides price subsidies have played an important role in reducing total fertility rates in developing countries. These other components include making modern contraceptive methods more easily accessible through improvements in a country's distribution network and health infrastructure, increasing the number of reproductive healthcare workers, educating couples about modern birth control, providing safe abortion services, and empowering women to bargain more effectively over the use of contraception.

Finally, this chapter has examined the mixed evidence on whether contraception and abortion are complements or substitutes. Is improved contraceptive access the best way to make abortions rarer? Not only is the evidence mixed, it is also rather sparse. Nonetheless, the answer to this question has hugely important policy implications, especially at a time when unsafe abortions are still a major cause of maternal morbidity and mortality abroad. The need for more evidence also comes at a time when antiabortion sentiment is driving public policy decisions and foreign aid flows around the globe. The remaining chapters delve deeper into these issues of public policies on abortion and the impact of changes in US family-planning assistance on abortion rates.

NOTES

1. UNDESA (2017) provides these data for 185 countries beginning with 1970. The six regional labels shown in Figure 4.1 and subsequent figures in this chapter represent aggregations of all 22 subregions in the UNDESA database, as follows: (1) "Sub-Saharan Africa" is eastern, western, southern, and middle Africa; (2) "Latin America and the Caribbean" is Central America, South America, and the Caribbean; (3) "South and Southeast Asia" is southern, eastern, and southeastern Asia, as well as Melanesia, Micronesia, and Polynesia; (4) "Eastern Europe and Central Asia" is Eastern Europe and Central Asia; (5) "Middle East and North Africa" is western Asia and Northern Africa; and (6) "Developed Countries" is Australia and New Zealand, Northern America, Western Europe, Southern Europe, and Northern Europe.

2. For some countries, UNDESA included multiple estimates of the total fertility rate in a particular year due to the availability of multiple sources of data and estimation methods. In these cases, I simply used the median total fertility rate in a particular year for that country.

3. As is often the case with economic modeling, assumptions and abstractions make these fertility models tractable and help to generate testable hypotheses. This tractability comes at a cost, which is the failure to portray the institutional contexts in which households operate, the constraints that women face in their decision-making within the household, women's philosophical views, and the role of culture and politics in reproductive life. Feminist social scientists have developed alternative approaches to fertility that situate women's reproductive behaviors in these broader contexts. See especially Folbre (1983), Greenhalgh (1995), and Jaffré and Suh (2016).

4. The examples listed here are motivated by accounts in Goldberg (2009) and the Economist (2016).

5. The literature on women's fertility and the role of contraception and family planning is voluminous. The discussion that follows is intended to give a sense of the range of estimates, from virtually no impact to substantially large impacts on women's fertility. For more comprehensive reviews and evidence, see Bryant (2007), Guinnane (2011), Bongaarts, Cleland, Townsend, Bertrand, and Das Gupta (2012), and Miller and Babiarz (2016).

6. There are also very few studies examining the substitutability between contraception and abortion in wealthy countries. Exceptions are Ananat and Hungerman (2012), Glasier et al. (2004), and Durrance (2013), each of which found either a small degree of substitutability or none at all.

Chapter 5

Global Abortion Policies
and Practices

Abortion practices and laws restricting them have existed since ancient times. The Egyptians, Romans, and Greeks were among the first to develop techniques for terminating unwanted pregnancies (Devereux, 1976). These techniques were predominantly nonsurgical and included engaging in strenuous physical activities, pouring hot water on the abdomen, lying on a heated coconut shell, fasting, bloodletting, and ingesting various herbs and medicinal plants. Texts from preindustrial cultures indicate that abortion was often considered a crime, subject to various punishments, including fines, imprisonment, and even the death penalty. By the early 1800s, abortion practices had modernized and included surgical procedures with appropriate sanitation and anesthesia. Laws that criminalized abortion also appeared during this period, with England passing legislation in 1803 that outlawed abortion and cited the death penalty as a possible punishment (although this form of punishment was dropped by 1840). The United States was not far behind in passing antiabortion legislation, but the punishment was generally less severe (Doan, 2007).

By the mid-1800s, abortions were being performed fairly frequently within and outside of the United States, and this remains true through the current period. In 2014, 56.3 million induced abortions were performed globally, up from 50.4 million in 1990 (Sedgh et al., 2016). Although the overall abortion rate fell during this period, the total number of abortions performed has risen over time due to population growth. Approximately one-quarter of all pregnancies globally ended in abortion in 2014, making abortion one of the most common gynecological practices worldwide. Despite this historical precedent and global prevalence, women still have very different experiences with abortion around the world. Women in higher-income economies generally have greater access to safe abortions. In contrast, women in lower-income countries experience greater health risks in getting abortions: in 2008, approximately 21.6 million unsafe induced abortions took place globally, almost all of them in developing countries (WHO, 2011). An unsafe abortion is defined by the World Health Organization as a procedure for terminating an unplanned pregnancy that is carried out either by someone who lacks the required skills or in a setting that does not meet minimal medical standards, or both. Also in 2008, 47,000 women died from unsafe abortions. Although this number of abortion-related deaths is high, it has declined considerably since 1990, when a staggering 546,000 maternal deaths were attributed to unsafe abortions (WHO, 2011). These deaths and complications are entirely preventable by investing more in maternal healthcare services, filling the unmet need for modern contraceptive methods, and improving women's access to safe abortion.

That said, access to affordable abortion services performed by trained professionals in sterile environments is limited in numerous countries because of lower levels of economic development as well as abortion laws that restrict women's access to safe abortions. In order to better understand the extent to which women are constrained by the state in obtaining a full range of reproductive health services, this chapter examines abortion rates around the world and how those rates vary according to national legislation on access to abortion. Abortion laws have a long history that has often been shaped by deeply entrenched religious views, political ideologies, and patriarchal structures. These ideologies in turn are closely intertwined with stigmas around abortion in which women who seek one are viewed as straying from feminine ideals that include women's natural fecundity, the irrevocability of their roles as mothers, and their instinctive nurturance of those who need care (Kumar, Hessini, and Mitchell, 2009).

Abortion stigmas vary according to local contexts and can contribute to the perpetuation of restrictive abortion legislation that can have the unintended consequence of increasing rather than decreasing abortion rates.

There is no definitive evidence that legal restrictions on abortions result in fewer abortions. If anything, countries with more restrictive abortion policies have more unsafe abortions, and countries that legalize abortions see a shift from clandestine, unsafe abortions to legal, safe abortions without an increase in abortion rates. Legalizing abortion is seen by a growing number of multilateral agencies, nongovernmental organizations, scholars, and advocates as a necessary step toward reducing unsafe abortions and improving women's reproductive health. Yet despite this authoritative shared view that access to safe, legal abortion is a fundamental right for women, more than 60 countries still ban abortion completely or only permit it to save the woman's life. This chapter explores more closely the historical legacy of abortion laws around the world, why restrictive policy regimes have persisted in some countries and have been liberalized in others, and how the laws are associated with women's reproductive health outcomes. Abortion restrictions, unmet need for contraception, stigma, and inadequate reproductive health services are a potent mix, with life-threatening outcomes for women that can be prevented with policy reforms that not only safeguard women's health but also promote their dignity and worth.

ABORTION LAWS AROUND THE WORLD

Legislation on abortion varies substantially across countries, from the complete criminalization of all abortions in six predominantly Catholic countries to abortion upon request in countries as diverse as Cambodia, Nepal, Belgium, and the United States (UNDESA, 2015b). Countries with no restrictions are largely found in the global North, while countries with the most restrictions tend to be in the global South, especially in Latin America and the Caribbean and in sub-Saharan Africa. Abortion is completely prohibited or only permitted to save a woman's life in 66 countries, accounting for roughly one-quarter of the world's population. In contrast, 61 countries accounting for about 40% of the world's population allow women to have an abortion without restriction as to the reason (Center for Reproductive Rights, 2014). This distribution in the number of countries permitting abortion on particular grounds has shifted over time. In 1996, only 24% of countries allowed abortion on request compared to 30% of countries two decades later, and more countries either banned abortion completely or only permitted it on the grounds of saving the woman's life (UNDESA, 2014). Note that most countries that do allow abortion without restriction have gestational limits of 12 weeks, and quite a few countries in this category also require parental authorization or notification. A few countries—notably the United States, Australia, and Mexico—have national legislation on abortion but allow abortion restrictions to vary at the state level. Accordingly, abortion law covering most people in the United States includes gestational limits of 14 weeks and requires parental authorization or notification.

A number of countries also have national policies that restrict access to contraception. Of the 186 countries for which UNDESA (2015b) provides information on contraceptive policies, there are 151 countries with no restrictions and 35 countries with at least one restriction on access to contraception. Numerous countries have multiple restrictions. The most common restriction is parental consent for minors (16 countries), followed by marital status (10 countries), minimum age (9 countries), emergency contraceptive pills (9 countries), sterilization of men (8 countries), and sterilization of women (5 countries). For sterilization, the restrictions are often that the procedure is forbidden as a means of contraception but may be allowed for therapeutic or medical reasons. In some cases, voluntary sterilization for contraceptive reasons requires spousal permission or notification, usually that of the husband for a wife's sterilization. Interestingly, there are just a few nations with three or more restrictions, and each of these is either majority Muslim or majority Catholic: Indonesia, Ireland, the Philippines, Jordan, and Vatican City. Vatican City is the only state that has all six restrictions. This policy on contraceptive access reflects the Catholic Church's long-term position on the use of modern contraception as being unnatural and sinful.

LEGISLATIVE HISTORY ACROSS REGIONS: SALIENT FEATURES

The use of national legislation to restrict women's access to abortion and contraception has a long history that varies considerably across regions largely because of ideological considerations associated with religious and political institutions. This legislative history has contributed to traditional views, stigmas, and social norms around abortion that are deeply ingrained and slow to change. While providing a detailed account of the history of abortion policy around the globe is beyond the scope of this book, it is fruitful to explore the salient features of abortion-policy regimes that distinguish the major developing regions (Eastern Europe, Latin America and the Caribbean, Africa, and Asia). These features help to explain why abortion rates vary so much across regions and why there may be spatial patterns in the effects of cuts in US assistance for family-planning and reproductive health services.

Interestingly, in 1920 the Russian Soviet Republic became the first country in the world to legalize abortion and to provide free abortion services in hospitals. The Ukraine and the rest of the Soviet Union similarly made abortion available on broad grounds shortly thereafter. However, in subsequent decades the government imposed several waves of restrictions and even a complete ban from 1936 to 1955 as part of Joseph Stalin's initiative to promote population growth and family values (Randall, 2011). Following Stalin's death, the Soviet government passed new abortion legislation in 1955 lifting the ban and again allowing women to obtain an abortion upon request. According to the preamble to the 1955 Soviet decree, this policy decision was rooted not only in public health objectives (such as the rationale of limiting "the harm caused to the health of women by abortions performed outside of hospitals") but also in ideological principles (such as the desire to give women "the possibility of deciding themselves the question of motherhood") (Frejka, 1983, 495). Most Eastern European countries followed suit in 1956 and 1957 with legislation that liberalized access to abortion. Abortion was widely considered in the region, both within and outside of the medical field, to be safer and cheaper than modern contraceptives (Westoff, Sharmanov, Sullivan, and Croft, 1998). Moreover, the government's failure to ensure sufficient contraceptive supplies effectively made abortion a form of birth control (Randall, 2011).

Subsequent rapid and unexpected fertility declines that some governments associated with the liberalization of abortion laws led countries such as Bulgaria, Czechoslovakia, Hungary, and Romania to reimpose abortion restrictions during the 1960s. In an effort to reverse declining fertility, some governments even combined these regulations with economic incentives for women to have children. Overall though, the decades since Russia's abortion liberalization saw widespread use of abortion as a method of fertility control, especially after 1980, when vacuum-aspiration became more prevalent to perform so-called miniabortions of very early pregnancies. Only after the collapse of Communism did abortion rates begin to fall in Eastern Europe and the former Soviet republics as modern contraceptive methods, especially intrauterine devices and birth control pills, became more widely available and accepted as safe and cost-effective forms of fertility control (Westoff et al., 1998). That said, Eastern European and Central Asian countries still stand out today for having more liberalized abortion policies and greater social acceptance of abortion than other regions.

The opposite holds true for Latin America and the Caribbean, largely due to the influence of the Catholic Church. Since the 1980s, conservative groups within the Catholic Church have worked hard to ensure that abortion policy across Latin America reflects the Vatican's strict stand against abortion (Goldberg, 2009). At the same time, American antiabortion groups exerted pressure on governments across the region to criminalize abortion. Fighting against these efforts by local Catholic leaders and their supporters in the United States and in the Vatican were various women's groups and nongovernmental organizations who believed strongly that women's access to safe abortion was a fundamental human right. As part of their strategy, in 1990 several women's groups started the Day of Action for Access to Safe and Legal Abortion. Every year since then, on September 28, women across the region have marched and protested for the decriminalization of abortion, improved access to reproductive health services, and the end of stigmatization of women who obtain abortions.[1]

Despite the activism of the women's movement and support from multilateral organizations and sympathetic governments in Europe, powerful pressure from the Catholic Church has prevailed, and five countries in the region passed complete abortion bans during this period: Honduras, Nicaragua, El Salvador, Dominican Republic, and Chile. These countries joined Malta and Vatican City as the only seven countries globally to ban abortion in all circumstances, even in cases when the woman's life is in danger. As of late 2017 only one of these countries had dropped its complete abortion ban. In August 2017 Chile's constitutional court ruled that abortion would be allowed on the grounds of saving the woman's life, severe fetal impairment, and in cases of rape (BBC, 2017). Among other countries in the region, the most common abortion policy is to permit abortion only on the grounds of saving the woman's life. Just three countries and one city allow abortion upon request: Guyana, Uruguay, Cuba, and Mexico City.

Like Latin America and the Caribbean, Africa also has restrictive abortion laws and high rates of unsafe abortion. The root causes differ though, in that African abortion laws are linked to colonial constitutions dating back to the 1800s. Traditional views in the colonial codes regarding women's inferior status have trickled through to the current period and are often manifested in deep-seated cultural taboos about sex, reproductive health, and abortion. Along with these cultural taboos, the region's extreme poverty and slow economic development have prevented women from having sufficient access to maternal health services and safe abortions. The shortage of doctors in the public sector, the inability of women to afford abortions in the private sector, and the aversion by health-care workers in the public sector toward abortion have all contributed to the stigmatization of abortion and the lack of access to safe abortion services (Ngwena, 2010).

A story told by Ghana's former health minister, Dr. Eunice Brookman-Amissah, has been used in the media to illustrate how powerful these cultural taboos can be. One day in 1992, while Brookman-Amissah was working as a gynecologist in Ghana, the 14-year-old daughter of a family friend came in to her private practice to ask her for an abortion. Brookman-Amissah said she was outraged, called the child a "naughty girl," and sent her away. A few days later Brookman-Amissah found out that the man who had gotten the girl pregnant had taken her to a witch doctor for an abortion and she had died. The girl's death led Brookman-Amissah to seriously question her own views on abortion, the criminalization of abortions in Ghana's legal codes, and society's stigmatization of women who sought abortions. She ultimately became a leading advocate for women's reproductive health and rights, serving as Ghana's health minister in the late 1990s and later taking on the role of vice president for Africa at Ipas, a global nonprofit organization for women's reproductive health (Goldberg, 2009; Okeowo, 2011).

In large part due to the concerted efforts of advocates such as Brookman-Amissah and pressure from a growing number of civil society groups, in 2003 the African Union adopted the Protocol to the African Charter on Human and Peoples' Rights on the Rights of Women in Africa (commonly known as the Maputo Protocol). After being ratified by 15 member nations of the African Union, the protocol came into force in 2005, calling for African governments to guarantee women a comprehensive set of rights, including the right to sexual and reproductive health. Importantly, the protocol urges governments to protect women's reproductive rights by authorizing abortion in cases of rape and incest, when the life of the woman or fetus is at risk, or when the pregnancy endangers the mental and physical health of the woman. As of late 2017, 36 out of 54 member countries had signed and ratified the Maputo Protocol (ACHPR, 2017). The protocol has been hailed as innovative and groundbreaking, especially for the way it identifies abortion as a fundamental right in a document that considers reproductive health to be a human right (Ngwena, 2010). However, even countries that ratified the protocol have been slow to change their abortion laws, and in many countries abortion remains criminalized except in cases when the woman's life is in danger. Just three African countries have legalized abortion on all grounds: South Africa, Tunisia, and Cape Verde. If the goal is to eradicate unsafe abortions in the region, then more work is needed to reform domestic laws and improve women's access to reproductive healthcare services.

As for the fourth major region, Asia exhibits more variation in its history of abortion policies, largely due to differences in political and religious ideologies across countries. Many countries have a history of relatively liberal policies on abortions, but several countries have instituted complete bans or severe restrictions. These more restrictive countries include Indonesia (which is predominantly Muslim), the Philippines (which is predominantly Catholic), and Laos and Myanmar (which are both predominantly Buddhist). One salient feature that sets Asia apart from the other regions is the use of sex-selective abortion, especially in China and India, as a manifestation of a strong cultural preference for sons. Son preference in these countries has arisen from a number of cultural, economic, and institutional factors that have caused parents to favor boys over girls in fertility and childcare decisions. Sen (1989) first drew attention to the "missing women" problem with evidence of unusually high male-to-female population ratios in Asia. In addition to high rates of sex-selective abortions, these countries have seen higher infant mortality for children born later in the birth order, especially for girls, due to strict population control policies and parents' preferences for an ideal number of children. Historically, the absence of social-security policies for old age and relatively fewer employment opportunities for women reinforced the lower social value of women and girls.

China had a particularly strict family-planning program with its one-child policy, which was introduced in 1979 and not relaxed until 2015. Couples who violated this policy faced a variety of punishments, including monetary penalties, job losses, and forced abortion. In the early 1980s the Chinese government moved family planning from the Ministry of Health to its own administrative unit. Somewhat ironically, this administrative reshuffling wound up increasing funding for family planning at the expense of maternal and child health, and women were not able to receive reproductive healthcare services when they visited family-planning clinics (Chen and Standing, 2007). Also during the 1980s, advances in prenatal sex-testing technologies contributed to higher rates of sex-selective abortions and increases in male/female population ratios, especially in China and India but also in South Korea and Taiwan, where family-planning policies were not as strict (Goodkind, 1996). In China, ultrasonography technology was first introduced in 1979, with dissemination across healthcare clinics beginning in the early 1980s. By 2001, virtually every hospital and clinic in urban and rural China had ultrasound sex-discernment equipment (Chu, 2001). The introduction of this technology followed a similar pattern in India, although widespread dissemination across urban and rural areas took more time. Following the spread of this technology, prenatal sex determination and sex-selective abortions became widespread in South and East Asia, especially for second and subsequent pregnancies.

Already in the early 1990s, a number of stakeholders in government, nongovernmental organizations, and international agencies expressed alarm at the growing incidence of sex-selective abortion, as

well as female infanticide. A formal statement in the program of action adopted at the 1994 International Conference on Population and
Development in Cairo labeled these practices as "harmful and uneth-
ical," thus initiating more discussions and actual moves to ban prenatal
sex testing and sex-selective abortions (Goodkind, 1996). At present,
most countries in the region have legally banned these procedures, although enforcement and compliance remain incomplete. As noted in
Kabeer, Huq, and Mahmud (2014), the "missing women" problem in
these countries has been replaced by the problem of "missing daughters"
and the practice of aborting girls has continued into the current generation of mothers, especially in India.

GLOBAL ABORTION RATES

Globally, abortion rates have fallen over time, from 40 to 35 abortions per
1,000 women of reproductive age between 1990–1994 and 2010–2014.
Table 5.1, based on aggregate abortion rates published in Sedgh et al.
(2016), shows that most of this decline occurred in developed countries (from 46 to 27 abortions per 1,000 women), while the estimated
decline in developing countries (from 39 to 37) is much smaller and is
not statistically significant. In the face of the overall decline in abortion
rates, the absolute number of abortions considered unsafe according to
standards set by the World Health Organization remained high, with
close to 7 million women in developing countries receiving treatment for
abortion complications in 2012, up from 5 million in 2005 (Singh and
Maddow-Zimet, 2016). Of note, abortion rates declined across regions
except Latin America and Africa, the two regions with the most restrictive laws. Table 5.1 also indicates that the absolute number of abortions
increased during the period. All of this growth occurred in developing
countries, primarily due to population growth. Similarly, the percentage
of pregnancies ending in abortion also rose in developing countries (from
21% to 24%, with a particularly large increase in Latin America), while it
dropped considerably in developed countries (from 39% to 28%, with a
particularly large drop in Europe). Globally, an average of one-quarter of
all pregnancies ended in abortion in 2010–2014. Despite intense lobbying

Table 5.1 GLOBAL ESTIMATES OF INDUCED ABORTION, 1990–1994
AND 2010–2014

	No. of abortions annually (millions)		Abortion rate (per 1,000 women ages 15–44)		% of pregnancies ending in abortion	
	1990–94	2010–14	1990–94	2010–14	1990–94	2010–14
World	50.4	56.3	40	35	23	25
Developed countries	11.8	6.7	46	27	39	28
Developing countries	38.6	49.6	39	37	21	24
Africa	4.6	8.3	33	34	12	15
Asia	31.5	35.8	41	36	23	28
Latin America	4.4	6.5	40	44	23	32
North America	1.6	1.2	25	17	23	17
Europe	8.2	4.4	52	30	42	30
Oceania	0.1	0.1	20	19	16	16

Source: Sedgh et al. (2016).

efforts by antiabortion groups, strong pressure from several religious institutions, formidable stigmas surrounding abortion, and highly restrictive abortion laws in numerous countries, abortion remains a common gynecological phenomenon across the globe.

It is both interesting and important to look beyond these aggregate numbers and examine individual countries more closely. Within the United States, the average abortion rate has fallen quite rapidly. Between

2008 and 2014 alone, the abortion rate fell by 25%, from 19.4 abortions for every 1,000 women of reproductive age to 14.6 (Jones and Jerman, 2017). These rates can be used to predict the percentage of women who are expected to have an abortion during their reproductive years, a number that fell from 30% to 25% during this period. Hence one in every four women in the United States is expected to have an abortion before the age of 45. Jones and Jerman attribute the decline in abortion rates since 2008 to better access to contraception and changes in contraceptive methods, with more women relying on long-acting reversible contraceptives such as intrauterine devices and implants.

Published cross-country data on abortion rates for individual countries are not widely available, especially for developing countries. UNDESA (2014) does provide published data on abortion rates for about 70 individual countries around the world—both developed and developing—and this information is depicted in Figure 5.1 for the most recent year available. These rates are calculated using data on the total number of legally induced abortions in each country. In countries where abortion is illegal or highly restricted, the published numbers are likely to underrepresent actual induced abortion rates. Because low-income countries tend to have more restrictive abortion policies, data on legally induced abortion rates are either not available or are more subject to reporting bias.

The first chart in Figure 5.1 reports legally induced abortion rates in the transition economies of Eastern Europe and West Asia. Countries that stand out among the others for their relatively high rates include Russia (34.2 abortions per 1,000 women ages 15–44) and Georgia (32.3). These relatively high rates are consistent with the historical precedent of liberalized abortion policies and the general acceptance of abortion as a method of fertility control. At the opposite extreme are Poland (0.1 abortions per 1,000 women of reproductive age) and Qatar (1.2). In Poland, abortion was legal during the era of Communist rule. However, after the fall of the Soviet Union in 1989, abortion policy became much more restrictive largely due to the influence of the Catholic Church, the "most visible transnational actor" in the global abortion debate, and the overwhelming majority of Polish people who identified themselves as Catholic (Kulczycki, 1999). As recently as 2016 Polish legislators pushed a new law to completely ban abortion on all grounds, but the government

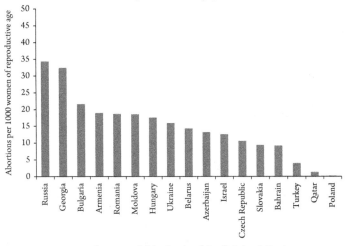

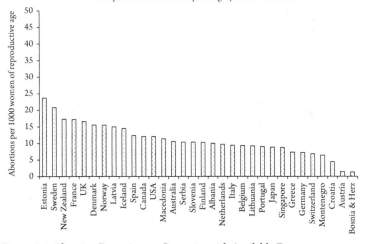

Figure 5.1 Abortion Rates Across Countries with Available Data

Source: Charts for legally induced abortions constructed with data in UNDESA (2014). Chart for all abortions constructed with data in Guttmacher Institute (2017a).

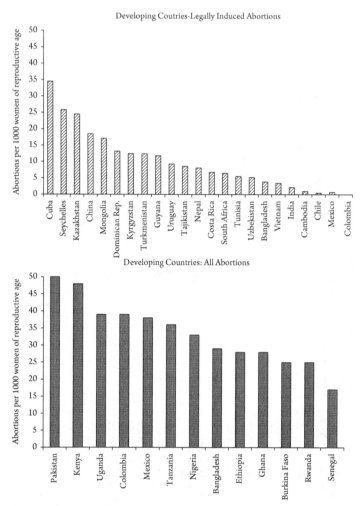

Figure 5.1 (Continued)

reversed its position on the proposed legislation after thousands of women marched in protest and went on strike across the country (Davies, 2016). News media sources suggest that the number of illegal abortions in Poland exceed the number of legal abortions by at least a factor of 10, but there are no official sources to verify these claims. There is even less information about estimated illegal abortion in Qatar, possibly because penalties for obtaining or performing an illegal abortion in Qatar are unusually high, with prison terms of up to 10 years (Atighetchi, 2007).

The second chart in Figure 5.1 shows legally induced abortion rates for a range of European countries and several other industrialized countries. Abortion rates for this group vary less than for the transition economies in Eastern Europe and West Asia. Estonia—classified by the United Nations as a northern European country despite its history as a Soviet republic—has the highest abortion rate in this group (23.7 abortions per 1,000 women of reproductive age), followed closely by Sweden. At the opposite end of the spectrum are Austria and Bosnia and Herzegovina, with rates just under 1.5 abortions per 1,000 women. All four of these countries have liberal abortion laws, and women have access to safe abortions. Estonia's relatively high rate is most likely explained by its legacy as a Soviet republic and the history of using abortion as a form of birth control. However, there is no systematic evidence explaining why abortions are relatively common in Sweden and so rare in Austria and in Bosnia and Herzegovina. Within this group of 32 countries, the United States has the twelfth highest abortion rate, at 12.1 abortions per 1,000 women of reproductive age, identical to that of Canada.[2]

Quite noticeable in the third chart of Figure 5.1 is the relatively small number of developing countries for which there are data on legally induced abortion rates, especially in Africa and in Latin America and the Caribbean. Cuba stands out from the rest with its relatively high rate of 34.5 abortions per 1,000 women ages 15–44, followed by Seychelles and Kazakhstan, each with abortion rates around 25. Cuba's abortion rate is one of the highest in the world. Not only is Cuba one of just a few countries in Latin America and the Caribbean to provide abortion upon request, it also has an "abortion culture" similar to other Soviet and post-Soviet countries in which abortion is used as a form of fertility control and people are generally skeptical of modern contraceptives (Bélanger and Flynn, 2009). At the opposite extreme, legally induced abortion rates are either zero or close to zero in Cambodia, Chile, Mexico, and Colombia. In the case of Cambodia, although abortion is legally available upon request, evidence in Fetters and Samandari (2015) indicates that the actual abortion rate was 28 abortions per 1,000 women ages 15–45 in 2010. This actual rate for Cambodia is considerably higher than the officially reported rate of 1 abortion per 1,000 women. The main explanation is that the majority of induced abortions are performed by women themselves or in the homes of untrained abortion providers (Fetters and Samandari, 2015).

The legally induced abortion rates in Chile, Mexico, and Colombia—where legal access to abortion is highly restricted—also misrepresent the true number of abortions being performed. Estimates published by the Guttmacher Institute indicate that actual abortion rates in these countries are considerably higher than legally induced abortion rates, and if anything they have been rising since the 1990s. This data source, which consists of a series of country fact sheets published for a small group of developing countries, was used to construct the fourth chart in Figure 5.1 showing actual abortion rates in the most recent year available during the 2000s. As seen in the chart, the actual abortion rate in Colombia is 39 abortions per 1,000 women of reproductive age, and in Mexico it is 38. The Guttmacher Institute estimated the rate in Chile to be 45 per 1,000 women of reproductive age in 1990, the last year for which data are available.

Actual abortion rates for the other developing countries shown in this chart are generally high as well, especially Pakistan (50 abortions per 1,000 women of reproductive age) and Kenya (48). According to the Guttmacher Institute, while abortion is legally allowed in Pakistan on the grounds of providing "necessary treatment," in practice the law has proven difficult to interpret and women have had trouble accessing legal abortion services. For this reason, most women in Pakistan wind up getting unsafe abortions from clandestine providers. Women in Kenya face a similar set of circumstances, resulting in higher abortion rates, more complications from unsafe abortions, and more abortion-related fatalities compared to most developing countries, including Kenya's neighbors in East Africa (Guttmacher Institute, 2017a). In comparison, the actual abortion rate of 16.9 abortions per 1,000 women of reproductive age in Senegal appears to be relatively low. According to the Guttmacher Institute, in Senegal abortion is completely banned in the criminal code but permitted under the code of medical ethics if three doctors testify it is necessary to save a woman's life. Findings in Suh (2017) based on an extensive set of interviews indicate that health workers in Senegal often misclassify postabortion care cases as miscarriages in order to avoid police intervention. To the extent that the Guttmacher Institute's estimate of 16.9 is subject to this misclassification bias, the actual abortion rate in Senegal is likely to be higher.

ASSOCIATION BETWEEN ABORTION POLICIES AND REPRODUCTIVE HEALTH

In the face of legislative bans and restrictions on abortion, the need for contraceptive services continues to outstrip supply, and recent estimates indicate that 214 million women in developing countries who want to prevent pregnancy do not have access to modern contraceptive methods. If all these women were to gain access to effective contraception, unintended pregnancies would fall by 67 million and unplanned births would fall by 23 million per year (Guttmacher Institute, 2017b). The conventional wisdom in policy and scholarly discourse is that the best way to decrease abortion rates is to prevent unwanted pregnancies. What works well is filling the unmet need for contraception, training health professionals in birth control counseling, and educating people about birth control methods. The efficacy of legally restricting access to abortion is far less clear. In fact, findings in Sedgh et al. (2016) show no association between abortion rates across countries and the legal status of abortion in those countries. If anything, abortion rates are slightly higher in countries that prohibit abortions altogether or allow them only to save a woman's life than in countries that allow abortion upon request.

A similar conclusion can be reached with evidence presented in UNDESA's (2014) report on abortion legislation and reproductive healthcare across countries. The report classifies countries into two groups according to the restrictiveness of their abortion laws: those that permit abortion on the grounds of economic or social reasons or on request are classified as having "liberal" abortion laws (70 countries), and the remaining countries are classified as having "restrictive" abortion laws (110 countries). The report then compares four indicators of women's reproductive health across these two categories using the most recently available data for each indicator: adolescent birth rates, total fertility rates, unsafe abortion rates, and maternal mortality ratios. As shown in Figure 5.2, each of these indicators is higher in countries with restrictive

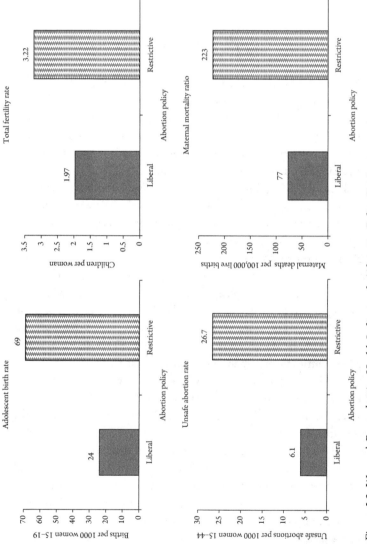

Figure 5.2 Women's Reproductive Health Indicators by Abortion Policy Regimes

Source: Constructed from data in UNDESA (2014).

abortion policies than in countries with more liberal abortion policies, usually by a substantial amount. More specifically, the average adolescent birth rate is 24 births per 1,000 women ages 15–19 in liberal abortion-law countries compared to 69 births per 1,000 adolescent women in restrictive countries. Moreover, the difference in average fertility rates is also large: 1.97 children per woman in liberal countries versus 3.22 children per woman in restrictive countries. These associations are of course correlations and largely reflect differences in economic development between the two groups (lower-income countries tend to have more restrictive abortion laws and higher fertility). We cannot, however, rule out a causal impact of restrictive abortion laws on fertility rates if the abortion restrictions cause women to have fewer options for terminating unplanned pregnancies.

Even larger in Figure 5.2 are the differentials between liberal and restrictive abortion-policy countries in unsafe abortion rates (6.1 versus 26.7 unsafe abortions per 1,000 women of reproductive age) and in maternal mortality rates (77 versus 223 maternal deaths per 100,000 live births). Again, these associations are correlations that largely reflect differences in economic development between the two categories of countries with restrictive versus liberal abortion policies. Many of the countries with restrictive abortion policies are less developed and have inadequate healthcare infrastructure and services, which is a direct contributor to unsafe medical procedures and maternal mortality. But there could be a causal impact if restrictive laws lead to fewer safe and reliable providers of abortion services, thus forcing women to resort to unsafe providers or self-induced abortion. This same argument would apply to maternal mortality rates since unsafe abortions cause a substantial proportion of maternal deaths.

Globally, almost 300,000 maternal deaths occur each year (Say et al., 2014; Kassebaum et al., 2014). In a comprehensive analysis of maternal mortality around the world using data from 2003 to 2009, Say et al. (2014) found that abortion accounts for a higher percentage of maternal mortality in Latin America and the Caribbean than in any other region, followed closely by sub-Saharan Africa. As shown in the first panel of Figure 5.3, 10% of all maternal mortality in Latin America and the Caribbean is caused by abortion. In contrast, abortion is found to cause less than 1%

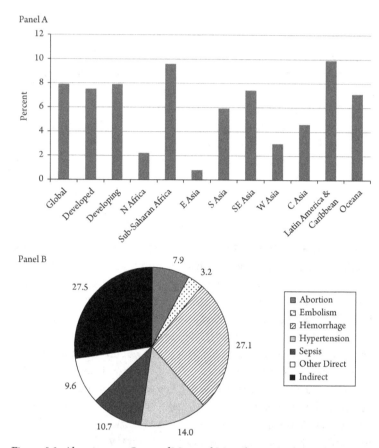

Figure 5.3 Abortion as a Cause of Maternal Mortality around the Globe
Panel A. Percentage of Maternal Mortality Caused by Abortion Across Regions
Panel B. Distribution of Causes of Maternal Mortality: Global Average
Source: Constructed from data in Say et al. (2014).

of maternal mortality in East Asia, a region with higher income and less restrictive abortion laws. Globally, the percentage of maternal deaths attributed to abortion is estimated to be 8% (Panel B), which is smaller than the top three direct causes of maternal mortality: obstetric hemorrhage (27%), hypertension disorders (14%), and pregnancy-related sepsis (11%). Note that deaths due to unsafe abortion may be even higher given the likely underreporting of abortion and the misclassification of abortion as hemorrhages and hypertension disorders (Gerdts, Vohra, and Ahern, 2013; Say et al., 2014).

These findings are broadly consistent with two other studies using alternative methods and data to examine the causes of maternal mortality across regions. Using data from 1998 to 2002, Khan, Wojdyla, Say, Gülmezoglu, and Van Look (2006) also found that abortion causes more maternal mortality in Latin America and the Caribbean than any other region. Among individual countries, maternal deaths due to abortion are particularly high in Argentina and Paraguay. The Khan et al. study argues that restrictive abortion laws are a major contributing factor toward the high incidence of unsafe abortions in the region. Similarly, Kassebaum et al. (2014) also found abortion to be one of the leading causes of maternal mortality. Data from 188 countries between 1990 and 2013 indicate that 15% of all maternal deaths globally can be attributed to abortions, with the highest percentage (21%) among all subregions in southern Latin America.

An important issue in this discussion of the association between abortion law and abortion rates is that a number of countries (especially those with lower national income) have limited capacities to enforce and implement legislation. This constraint is especially problematic when countries have moved to liberalize their abortion laws but the actual provision of services has been slow to respond (WHO, 2011). Countries transitioning from more restrictive to liberalized abortion laws may have insufficient health infrastructure or skilled practitioners to provide the services that have become legally permissible. Closely related, social norms and attitudes are often slower to change than legal statutes, so women may still be obtaining clandestine abortions even while legally allowed to do so, due to the stigma around abortion. Also affecting both service providers and women seeking abortions is insufficient knowledge about abortion law reforms or confusion about technical requirements. For example, a government may expand the grounds for abortion to include instances of rape or incest, but women who become pregnant for this reason may still get an unsafe abortion if they are unsure about whether or not they need a police report. Moreover, health providers in the area may refuse to perform an abortion because they are confused about reporting requirements or they fear legal reprisal.

The country case studies documented in Guttmacher Institute (2017a) suggest that this gap between abortion law liberalization and implementation can be substantial, resulting in the persistence of high numbers of unsafe abortions. One example is Kenya, which adopted a new constitution in 2010 that gave health professionals more leeway to perform abortions in cases when emergency treatment was needed or if the life or health of the woman was in danger. However, two years later Kenya still had some of the highest rates of severe complications from unsafe abortions and abortion-related fatalities in the region. It was not at all clear that the medical community understood the new law, Kenya's penal code had not yet been revised to reflect the new legislation, and many practitioners were still afraid to provide abortion services (Guttmacher Institute, 2017a).

Counteracting this failure of health infrastructure to keep up with legislative reform are improvements in reproductive-health technologies, the spread of the internet across developing countries, the availability of online information on reproductive health, and the ability to order abortion pills online. The widespread dissemination of information through the internet has helped to destigmatize both abortion and contraception and has provided healthcare practitioners and women with clinical information about fertility control and safe abortion procedures, including abortion pills (Crane, Daulaire, and Ezeh, 2017). Abortion pills are the popular name for medical abortions, which involve taking the medicine mifepristone (which stops the body from producing the hormones necessary for pregnancy) followed by misoprostol (which induces contractions). Mifepristone is also known as RU-486. Abortion pills were first developed and widely used in France in the 1980s before spreading to other countries. Among developing countries, some of the first trials were conducted in China, Cuba, and India, with results indicating that although there were more side effects from medical abortions than from surgical abortions, none of the side effects were serious and women were more satisfied with medical abortions (Winikoff et al., 1997). The authors concluded that medical abortion could be used as a safe, acceptable, and efficacious method in developing countries, calling this method a "revolutionary technique," (Winikoff et al., 1997, 437). A similar conclusion was reached following additional trials in other developing countries, including Elul et al.'s (2001) study of medical abortion in Vietnam and Tunisia. Elul and her coauthors emphasized a lower dosage of mifepristone than the typical European regimen and home-based administration of the follow-up drug misoprostol rather than clinic visits as a way to keep the process more affordable and feasible in developing countries.

Because medical abortions do not require the same health infrastructure as surgical abortions, access to safe abortion has become more feasible for women in developing countries. The World Health Organization approved the combination of mifepristone and misoprostol to induce abortion in the first 12 weeks of pregnancy, and it placed the drugs on its list of essential medicines in 2005. However, the use of these two drugs to perform medical abortions is still not a widely available option in developing countries. High prices and restrictive regulations, especially in the case of mifepristone, have limited the widespread use of medical abortions. By 2011, misoprostol was approved in over 80 countries, mostly for the prevention and treatment of gastric ulcers. However, mifepristone was only approved for abortion in 45 countries, most of them higher-income countries (Sneeringer, Billings, Ganatra, and Baird, 2012). Starting in 2006, a Dutch nonprofit organization named Women on Web started making mifepristone and misoprostol kits more accessible all over the world to women who otherwise did not have access to safe abortion. Women who order these kits, which include a pregnancy test and detailed instructions, must complete an online interactive medical consultation that is reviewed by a physician, and they are expected to comply with all laws and regulations of the countries where they live (Gomperts, Jelinska, Davies, Gemzell-Danielsson, and Kleiverda, 2008).

In many countries women often use misoprostol by itself, rather than in a combined regimen with mifepristone, because it is widely available from doctors, pharmacies, and the black market not only to treat ulcers but also postpartum hemorrhage. However, when used by itself, misoprostol may cause more side effects and incomplete abortions than when it is combined with mifepristone (Coelho et al., 1993). In these cases women often wind up seeing a healthcare provider for postabortion care services, especially manual vacuum aspiration (MVA) procedures to complete the abortion. A growing body of evidence indicates that the increased availability and affordability of misoprostol has made medical abortion more common. The fact that postabortion care services are usually exempted from national abortion laws (and from US funding restrictions) has meant that women can use misoprostol followed by postabortion care services if necessary to ensure that they have a complete abortion. Thus changes in abortion access and practice have contributed to increasing abortion rates in some countries in the face of highly restrictive national legislation.

Despite the growth of internet-based sources of abortion pills, there are still insufficient local providers of safe and effective medical abortions in developing countries. Calls for reform include more regulatory approvals for both drugs as well as improved training of pharmacists—often the first-line providers of medicines in developing countries—to provide more accurate information on dosage, mode of administration, side effects, and gestational limits (Sneeringer et al., 2012). Because surgical abortion is still such an explosive legal and social issue, some consider medical abortion the next frontier in safe abortion access—a scenario that will become realized as mifepristone and misoprostol become more widely available through the internet and through pharmacies.

Closely related to this discussion is the availability of emergency contraceptive pills online and through local pharmacies and health providers across countries. Emergency contraceptive pills (also known as morning-after pills and as Plan B, which is one of the brands) can stop a pregnancy before it starts if taken within five days after unprotected sexual intercourse or contraceptive failure.[3] Emergency contraceptive pills are often confused with abortion pills, but they are not the same thing. Emergency contraceptive pills work by preventing or delaying ovulation or fertilization, while abortion pills are taken after pregnancy has occurred. One reason for the confusion is that the drug mifepristone is found in both the abortion-pill regimen (as one of the two key drugs) and in one of the categories of emergency contraceptive pills (at a much lower dose). The use of low-dose mifepristone pills as emergency contraception has not been approved in the United States, while it has been approved in six other countries: China, Vietnam, Armenia, Moldova, Russia, and Ukraine (ICEC, 2017). The most common type of emergency contraceptive pills globally is progestin-only pills (such as the brand Plan B) that are sold over the counter in numerous countries, including the United States.

PAVING THE WAY FOR SAFE ABORTIONS

This chapter has presented descriptive evidence pointing to widespread restrictions on women's access to abortion services across developing regions. Yet despite the legal bans and restrictions, abortion remains prevalent across developing countries, and a substantial percentage of maternal mortality is attributed to unsafe abortions. No empirical study has found that restricted access to abortion has a statistically significant impact in reducing abortions. If anything, the descriptive statistics in this chapter suggest that countries with more legal restrictions actually have higher abortion rates and higher maternal mortality. The evidence also indicates that most abortions in countries with highly restrictive policies are unsafe and require postabortion care. It is thus very difficult to rationalize stronger abortion laws that further prevent women from accessing abortion services. The accumulated available evidence indicates that the best way to reduce maternal mortality due to unsafe abortion without raising abortion rates is to decriminalize abortion (Faúndes and Shah, 2015).

The countries that have seen the most rapid change in women's health indicators are those that have changed their laws at the same time that they have improved their service delivery. Nepal and Ethiopia are often cited as models for change. In 2002, Nepal's parliament legalized abortion on any grounds up through 12 weeks of gestation, in cases of rape or incest up though 18 weeks of gestation, and through any week of gestation if the woman's life is at risk. Before the law change, Nepal had one of the highest maternal mortality rates in the world, with a relatively high proportion of those deaths attributed to unsafe abortions. By 2004 the government had made safe abortion services readily available, including medical abortion, and it started a program to train healthcare providers, including nurses and midwives, to perform abortions. The program also included dissemination of information about the law change and locations for safe abortion services. Within an eight-year period, the maternal mortality ratio fell from 310 to 190 maternal deaths per 100,000 live births, one of the lowest among Asia's developing countries (PAI, 2015). Similarly, Ethiopia expanded its abortion law in 2005 to permit more conditions under which women could seek an abortion. At the same time the government invested in the country's health infrastructure—which included constructing new health centers and training health providers—to increase women's access to safe abortion services. Ethiopia also became one of the few African countries to legalize both misoprostol and mifepristone to perform medical abortions (Guttmacher Institute, 2017a).

Another example of a change in abortion law that has created a pathway to more safe abortions is the allowance of a "health exception" in which the term is interpreted more broadly to allow for the possibility of harm to the woman's health if the pregnancy continues; the woman need not necessarily be in imminent danger (González Vélez, 2012). An example often cited is Colombia, which in 2006 overturned its complete ban and decriminalized abortion on the grounds of endangerment to a woman's life or health, severe fetal abnormalities, and rape or incest, when certified by a medical doctor. However, even two years later, the new legal criteria had not been adequately disseminated to judges, doctors, and women. In 2008, there were approximately 400,400 induced abortions in Colombia, only 322 of which were recorded as legal procedures (Guttmacher Institute, 2017a). To promote more effective change, Colombia led the way for a number of other countries in Latin America to similarly adopt the health exception and create a regional forum to build a broader understanding of the health exception in a human rights framework. This forum led public health officials and members of civil society in 2009 to develop and disseminate a comprehensive set of training, advocacy, and counseling programs to help promote awareness of the legal interpretation of the new health exception. Evidence in González Vélez (2012) indicates that the number of legal abortions on the grounds of the health exception increased markedly in Colombia after the training programs started in 2009.

Medical practices are changing to create a middle ground in which women can seek a safe abortion in countries where abortion is still prohibited or highly restricted. A case in point is the risk and harm reduction strategy against unsafe abortion that was initially implemented in Uruguay and has been credited for achieving substantial reductions in unsafe abortions and maternal mortality. Harm reduction is a public health model that attempts to reduce the harms associated with an activity or behavior without attaching moral judgement to the behavior or sending it further underground. One of the most well-known examples is needle-exchange programs for intravenous drug users to prevent HIV transmission. Harm reduction was applied to safe abortion in Uruguay starting in 2001, when a small group of doctors developed a risk and harm reduction strategy that created a space in the health system for women with unwanted pregnancies who were likely to seek a high-risk abortion at a time when abortion was criminalized. The doctors gave the female patients information from the public domain that would allow them to make an informed decision about abortion. Patients were also given access to misoprostol so that at least they would undergo a lower-risk abortion (Labandera, Gorgoroso, and Briozzo, 2016). Other countries have since adopted this "Uruguay model" of information access through physician-patient counseling and self-administration of misoprostol in restrictive legal environments (Erdman, 2011). The program also wound up having a social and legal impact when the Uruguayan government legalized abortion in 2008, declaring that women with an unwanted pregnancy have the right as citizens to receive ethical treatment and dignity in the health system (Labandera et al., 2016).

As noted in Grimes et al. (2006, 1908), "The underlying causes of morbidity and mortality from unsafe abortion today are not blood loss and infection but, rather, apathy and disdain toward women." This assessment of unsafe abortion highlights the importance of addressing the social determinants of health, in addition to the medically oriented factors. Examples include laws, social norms, and customary practices that impoverish and disempower women, including violence against women. Empirical studies point to an association between violence against women and poor maternal health, while women who are empowered with property rights face less domestic violence (Panda and Agarwal, 2005). These social determinants of maternal health provide a strong rationale for a broader approach to reproductive health that includes legal and economic empowerment of women rather than restrictions on their access to safe abortion.

NOTES

1. This Day of Action, which is still held annually on September 28, expanded to the global level beginning in 2011.
2. This estimate for the United States is about 2.5 percentage points lower than the estimate in Jones and Jerman (2017) due to differences in the underlying data and methodology.
3. In addition to pills, emergency contraception also takes the form of intrauterine devices.

Chapter 6

Impact of the Global Gag Rule

New Estimates

This chapter offers new estimates of how the global gag rule has affected abortion rates across developing countries in four regions: Latin America and the Caribbean, Eastern Europe and Central Asia, South and Southeast Asia, and sub-Saharan Africa.[1] The chapter uses a statistical approach to assess the relationship between abortion rates and the global gag rule, based on data for individual women across countries in each of these regions. The methodology centers on regression analysis, which allows the researcher to control for other variables that could also affect changes in abortion rates. It also allows the researcher to determine if the association between abortion rates and the global gag rule is statistically significant (that is, not due to chance). By way of a brief summary, the dependent variable (whether or not a woman has an induced abortion) is regressed on a set of independent variables thought to explain the likelihood of having an abortion. The key independent variable of interest is a measure of a country's exposure to the global gag rule, and other independent variables include controls for women's characteristics that influence their decision-making around abortion, such as their education and marital status. The regressions also include country-level control variables that influence the incidence of abortions, such as national abortion laws and the prevalence of modern contraceptive use.

The regression analysis follows a "difference in difference" strategy that is commonly used in statistical analyses to estimate the impact of a policy change or a new program. In such a strategy, the policy impact is identified by looking at a particular indicator and calculating how that in-dicator differs between a group that experienced the policy (the treatment group) and a group that did not experience the policy (the control group), as well as the difference in the indicator before and after the policy was implemented. In this case, the chapter estimates the impact of the global gag rule by calculating the difference in abortion rates between women in countries that were more vulnerable to USAID funding restrictions versus women in countries that were less vulnerable, and the difference in abortion rates before and after the global gag rule was enacted. This analysis builds on two previous studies that have used statistical methods to examine the impact of the global gag rule on abortion rates in sub-Saharan Africa: Bendavid, Avila, and Miller (2011) and Jones (2015). By examining a broader range of countries, this chapter addresses the impor-tant question of how the US funding restrictions impacted abortion rates in regions besides sub-Saharan Africa.

The main finding is that the global gag rule is associated with a very large increase in abortion rates in Latin America and the Caribbean. In this region, women in countries that were highly exposed to the global gag rule had more than three times the odds of having an abortion after the global gag rule was reinstated in 2001 compared to women in less-exposed countries and before the reinstatement of the policy. This effect is even larger than it is for sub-Saharan Africa, where women in highly exposed countries had about twice the odds of having an abortion after the 2001 reinstatement of the policy compared to women in less-exposed countries and before the policy was reinstated. Abortion rates rose in both these regions despite their very restrictive legal regimes around abortion. In contrast, the relative odds of having an abortion declined for women in the other two regions (in Eastern Europe and Central Asia, and in South and Southeast Asia) in highly exposed coun-tries after the reinstatement of the policy, even though both these re-gions have more legal grounds upon which women are allowed to obtain abortions. In Eastern Europe and Central Asia the decline was com-pletely offset by the greater odds of getting an abortion due to increased funding from other donor countries. The results point to another inter-esting finding, and that is the lack of a conclusive and consistent relation-ship between strict abortion laws and women's likelihood of having an abortion. Overall then, women in Latin America and sub-Saharan Africa bore relatively more of the burden of the US restrictions on funding for family planning and reproductive health than women in other regions. This result helps to fill a knowledge gap on the global impact of the US funding restrictions.

The regressions used to derive these results are estimated with a comprehensive data set of about 6.3 million women across 51 countries over the 1994–2008 period. This data set contains information on women's reproductive health history, as well as relevant characteristics specific to the individual women and the countries where they live. The remainder of this chapter discusses in more detail the data set construction, the empirical methodology, and the statistical results on how the global gag rule is associated with abortion rates across regions.

INDUCED ABORTION RATES: DATA CHALLENGES

The first step in the analysis was to calculate induced abortion rates across countries and over time. Unfortunately, it is difficult to obtain reliable data on abortion rates in developing countries, mostly because the reporting systems are inadequate or because women are reluctant to disclose in surveys that they have had an abortion, or some combination of both of these factors (Westoff, 2008). Moreover, there are no readily available data on induced abortion rates that have been calculated using comparable methods across countries and covering an extensive time period. To address this problem I followed the approach used in Bendavid et al. (2011) and constructed induced abortion rates using household-level data from the Demographic and Health Surveys (DHS). The DHS are large nationally representative household surveys that provide a wealth of information on population, health, and nutrition in developing countries. The DHS program is administered by a private firm (ICF International) and is funded mostly by USAID, along with contributions from other donors and participating countries. The data are publicly available and are widely used in scholarly research on the well-being of women and their families. To date, there are surveys available for over 90 developing countries, and for many of those countries the DHS program has conducted surveys in multiple years—typically once every five years for a standard survey.

The DHS data are not without their limitations, especially the potential biases resulting from reporting and recall errors among survey respondents. However, previous assessments of the DHS indicate that most information is reasonably well reported (even information about events in the past such as children's birthdates and age at marriage), and that the benefits of using DHS data far outweigh the limitations (Boerma and Sommerfelt, 1993). The nationally representative sampling techniques and well-substantiated methodology have contributed to the DHS's reputation for providing accurate data on a range of population and health topics, including reproductive health, family-planning practices, household structures, and birth histories. Moreover, common questionnaire formats and variable coding across countries make the DHS data conducive for engaging in research that covers multiple countries. Because the DHS questionnaires are extensive and contain information on all members of a household, the DHS data for each country are separated into several "recodes" that are specific to certain categories, including women, men, children, household, and births. For each country examined in this chapter, data construction started with the DHS Individual Recode, which contains observations for women ages 15–49.

The key criterion for including a particular country in the analytic sample for this chapter was whether the DHS for that country included a calendar related to women's reproductive health history in the five to six years leading up to the date of the survey interview. The DHS program began to collect this calendar information in the early 1990s with the third wave of its standard survey in a few countries—including Turkey, Bolivia, and Zimbabwe—and the calendar has since become a standard part of the data collection efforts for many of the DHS program countries but not all. Any country in the DHS program that did not include a calendar on women's reproductive health was excluded from the analytic sample for this chapter, as was any country that did not have calendar information available for the period of analysis.[2] This exclusion restriction resulted in an analytic sample that covers a total of 51 countries: 9 countries in

Latin America and the Caribbean; 12 countries in Eastern Europe and Central Asia; 10 countries in South and Southeast Asia; and 20 countries in sub-Saharan African (see Table A6.1). The analytic sample was further restricted to women between the ages of 15 and 44 in each year.

A typical calendar for each woman interviewed in the survey includes monthly entries starting with the month of the survey interview and extending back in time for five or six years. Each monthly entry notes one of the following: whether the woman was using birth control and what kind (usually indicated by a single-digit number depending on the type of method and the country of the survey), whether the woman was pregnant (P), whether the woman experienced a termination (T), or whether the woman gave birth (B). A sample calendar entry is shown below:

11BPPPPPPPP0055555555555555555555BPPPPPPPP005555
55555TPP9999999999

The entry is read from right to left, where the rightmost character is the status of a woman's reproductive health in January five years before the survey, and the leftmost character is the woman's status during the month she completed the interview for the survey. In this particular example, reading from right to left, the woman was using the withdrawal method (a code of 9 in this sample country) five years before the survey, after which she was pregnant for two months and then experienced a termination. She then switched to a different birth control method (code 5, which represents condom) for almost a year and then stopped using any birth control (0) and became pregnant again. In this case the pregnancy was carried to term, and, following the birth, the woman continued to use condoms for over a year. She then stopped using birth control and became pregnant again and had another child. Following the second child, she switched to a different birth control method, in this case the pill (a code of 1), and was using this form of birth control the month she was interviewed for the survey. Each of these monthly entries in the single string was parsed to form separate codes, and then the codes were tabulated to construct a variable for whether or not a woman had experienced a termination (T) in a particular year.

The calendar does not specify if the termination was induced or spontaneous, nor is there other information in the standard DHS data sets across countries that specifically indicate the reason for each termination. Hence additional steps were necessary to calculate induced abortion rates. The methodology used in this chapter followed closely that of Bendavid et al. (2011), which in turn is based on a classification scheme developed in Magnani, Rutenberg, and McCann (1996). This scheme uses information on contraceptive use, family planning, pregnancy duration, and the age and marital status of the mother. In sum, a termination (T) in the DHS calendar is categorized as an induced abortion if any one of the following three conditions of the terminated pregnancy hold: (1) the pregnancy happened due to contraceptive failure, or (2) the pregnancy was unwanted (as indicated by answers to questions about the desired number of children and about the previous live birth), or (3) the woman was under the age of 25 and single at the time of the pregnancy. Even if one of those conditions is met, a termination is not considered an induced abortion if (a) the termination occurred during the third trimester, or (b) the woman indicated she stopped using contraception in order to become pregnant, or (c) the woman had no children at the time of the termination and was either married or in a union. These additional three criteria help to avoid falsely classifying a spontaneous termination as an induced abortion. As discussed in Bendavid et al. (2011) and in Magnani et al. (1996), this procedure is reliable—as indicated by robustness tests comparing the results from the algorithm with results from direct survey questions—and it is useful because it facilitates the calculation of abortion rates across multiple countries using the same methodology.

Table A6.1 reports the number of induced abortions calculated from the DHS data for each of the 51 countries in each year, as well as the total number of observations. The data span 1994 to 2008, with the 1994–2000 subperiod covering years in which the global gag rule was not in place and the 2001–2008 subperiod covering years in which the global gag rule was in place. Recall that the global gag rule was rescinded by President Bill Clinton in 1993, reinstated by President George W. Bush in 2001, and rescinded again by President Barack Obama in 2009. The datapoints are at the level of women per year. Thus, as an example from the table, in 1994 there were a total of 6,593 women in the sample for Bolivia, and 16 of them had an induced abortion in that year. Many countries have missing values for at least one of the years because not all of the DHS surveys included calendars or because the countries did not engage in regular waves of data collection during the entire period of analysis.

Table A6.1 shows that among the four regions, induced abortions occur more frequently in Eastern Europe and Central Asia, with some of the highest levels and rates found in Armenia, Azerbaijan, and Kazakhstan— each a former Soviet republic where attitudes, norms, and laws around abortion have been relatively less restrictive. In Armenia, almost 60 of every 1,000 women in the DHS samples during the middle to late 1990s had an induced abortion. In contrast, induced abortions are the least common in both absolute and relative terms in sub-Saharan Africa, corresponding to the region's stronger stigmas and laws surrounding access to abortion. Benin, Burkina Faso, Guinea, Mali, and Niger had particularly low incidences of induced abortions over time, with zero induced abortions in the DHS samples in some of the years. In between these two regions in terms of the incidence of induced abortions are South and Southeast Asia, as well as Latin America and the Caribbean. India and Colombia stand out for their particularly high numbers of induced abortions in absolute terms due to their large populations and sample sizes, and Timor Leste stands out at the opposite extreme with virtually no induced abortions in the sample.

MEASURING EXPOSURE TO THE GLOBAL GAG RULE

The next step in the analysis was to merge into the induced-abortions database a variable that measures exposure to the global gag rule. This country-level variable was constructed from data extracted from the Creditor Reporting System of the Organization for Economic Cooperation and Development (OECD, 2017). More specifically, for each country in the sample, data were extracted on total US commitments of official development assistance in current US dollars for family-planning and reproductive health services from 1995 to 2000. In the original source data, family planning is sector 13030 and reproductive health is sector 13020. I added these two items together to calculate assistance for family-planning and re-productive health services. The motivation behind the choice of years was to measure the extent to which developing countries depended on US fi-nancial support before the global gag rule was reinstated in 2001. The year 1995 is the earliest year for which the OECD reports these data, and the year 2000 is the final year during the Clinton administration when the global gag rule was not in place. Moreover, this OECD database is the only readily available database on detailed indicators of public financial assistance for global health across all developing countries going back historically to the mid-1990s. USAID and nonprofit organizations such as the Kaiser Family Foundation provide a number of published summary reports on US gov-ernment assistance for family-planning and reproductive health services, but these reports do not include data that are disaggregated by recipient country, and their scope in terms of historical coverage is limited.

The annual US financial assistance for each country was then con-verted into per capita terms by dividing the annual dollar amounts by that country's total population in the corresponding years using data from the World Bank's World Development Indicators (World Bank, 2017). Following the approach in Bendavid et al. (2011), the next step in constructing the exposure variable was to calculate the average per capita financial assistance over the 1995–2000 period for each country. That step resulted in 51 average financial-assistance datapoints (one for each country) spread across four regions. For each region I then computed the median amount of these average financial-assistance datapoints. The final step was to create a dichotomous variable (a variable that takes on only two possible values) in which countries with average per capita financial assistance from the United States that ranked above the median for their region are considered to have high exposure to the global gag rule, and countries with average per capita financial assistance from the United States that ranked below the median for their region are considered to have low exposure to the global gag rule. Countries above the median were assigned the value of 1, and countries below the median were assigned the value of 0, resulting in a "dummy variable" for whether or not a country was highly exposed to the global gag rule.

Figure 6.1 illustrates the ranking of countries according to their av-erage per capita assistance for family-planning and reproductive health

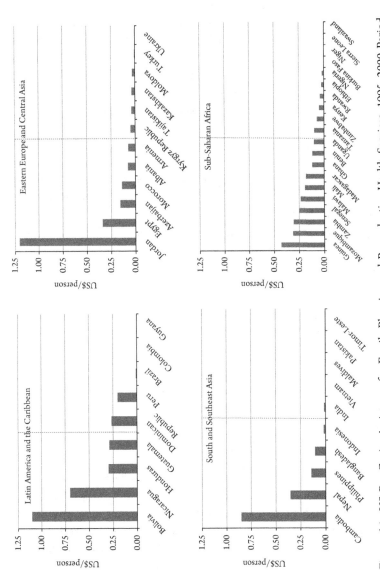

Figure 6.1. US Per Capita Assistance for Family-Planning and Reproductive Health Services, 1995–2000 Period Average

services from the United States for the 1995 to 2000 period, by region. In each of the four charts, a vertical line at the center divides the countries categorized as high exposure (those to the left of the line) from the countries categorized as low exposure (those to the right of the line). Note that each chart uses the same range of values for the vertical axes, so one can readily see which countries around the world received the most and the least per capita assistance from the United States. That said, both Jordan and Bolivia stand out for having per capita financial assistance that far exceeds all the other sample countries. One can speculate that these two countries are such outliers in terms of assistance from the United States due to political reasons, but there is no readily available source of information to substantiate this conjecture. Cambodia and Nicaragua also have fairly high levels of per capita assistance from the United States. These four countries thus had the highest relative exposure to the reinstatement of the global gag rule in 2001. At the other extreme, several countries in each region received zero official development assistance for family-planning and reproductive health services from the United States during the period.

OTHER DETERMINANTS OF ABORTION RATES

The regression analysis includes several additional independent variables that also influence women's abortion rates. Four of these variables represent characteristics of individual women in each year during the 1994–2008 period, and they were constructed with data from the DHS. The individual characteristics include the following: a woman's age in each year, a dummy variable for whether or not a woman has formal schooling, a dummy variable for whether or not a woman has been married, and a dummy variable for whether or not she lives in an urban area. Table A6.2 reports the sample averages for each of these variables.[3] Across the four regions, women's averages ages range from about 27 to 29. The regions exhibit greater variation in the other indicators, with less than 60% of women in sub-Saharan Africa having any kind of formal schooling, compared to at least 70% in the other regions. Women in sub-Saharan Africa also stand out for their relatively low tendency to live in urban areas (28%) compared to the other regions. In contrast, the region comprising Latin America and the Caribbean stands apart for its high incidence of women who never married—25%, at least double that in the other regions.

Four additional independent variables are included in the model to control for country-level characteristics for each year in the 1994–2008 period that may influence abortion decisions. Note that each of these indicators was merged in as panel data—that is, the indicators for each country were merged in for each year of the 1994–2008 period. The alternative would have been to assume that the country indicators did not change over time and could be represented by a period average or by a particular year of data. Because the regression models include country fixed effects, any country-level indicator needs to vary over time or else it gets dropped from the regression estimations due to multicollinearity. The first control variable measures a country's total life expectancy at birth in every year from 1994 to 2008 and was constructed using data from the World Development Indicators (World Bank, 2017). This variable is included as an indicator of a country's overall well-being as well as fertility patterns. The second country-level variable is the prevalence of modern contraceptives in each country, constructed with data from the Estimates and Projections of Family Planning Indicators Database of the United Nations Department of Economic and Social Affairs (UNDESA, 2017). These data indicate the percentage of married or in-union women of reproductive age who report that they use a modern method of contraception. Modern methods include sterilization, birth control pills, intrauterine devices, condoms, injectables, implants, vaginal barrier methods, and emergency contraceptives.

The third country-level indicator is an index that measures legal restrictions on access to abortions across countries. These data are obtained from the World Population Policies Database of the United Nations Department of Economic and Social Affairs (UNDESA, 2015b). For each country, this database indicates the legal grounds on which abortion is allowed. These grounds are, from most restrictive to least restrictive: (1) to save a woman's life, (2) to safeguard a woman's physical health, (3) to protect a woman's mental health, (4) when pregnancy is the result of rape or incest, (5) for reasons of fetal impairment, (6) for economic or social reasons, and (7) on request. Following the procedure described in Bloom, Canning, Fink, and Finlay (2009), rather than specify these legal grounds as separate measures, they are combined into an aggregate index that gives equal weight to each measure. Each of the legal grounds is assigned a value of 1 and then these values are simply added together, resulting in an index that ranges from 0 to 7. A score of 0 indicates that a country bans abortions entirely, and a score of 7 indicates that a country allows abortions for all the legal grounds given above. Note that the population polices in the original UNDESA source are not provided for every year of the period of analysis. Rather, the policy data are provided for the years 1996, 2001, 2003, 2005, and 2007. To construct annual series for each country, I worked forward from each year of the published policies. Thus the 1996 reported policies were assumed to apply to the years 1996–2000, the 2001 reported policies were assumed to apply to the years 2001–2002, the 2003 reported policies were assumed to apply to the years 2003–2004, and similarly for the 2005 and 2007 policies.

The fourth country-level indicator is the level of financial assistance for family-planning and reproductive health services from all other OECD donor countries besides the United States, given that other countries also committed substantial amounts of aid during the period. These data come from the Creditor Reporting System of the Organization for Economic Cooperation and Development (OECD, 2017). For each country in the sample, data were extracted on total non-US commitments of official development assistance in current US dollars for family-planning and reproductive health services from 1995 to 2008. Because the OECD source does not report foreign aid flows prior to 1995, to complete the analytic sample, data for the year 1994 were constructed using a simple linear interpolation. As before, the total non-US financial assistance for family-planning and reproductive health services to each country was converted into per capita terms using population data from the World Bank (2017).

Sample means for these country-level indicators are also found in Table A6.2. Notably, average life expectancy at birth is substantially lower in sub-Saharan Africa (52) than in the other regions, where it ranges from 66 to 70. Driving down the average in sub-Saharan Africa are very low life expectancies in countries that have been particularly hard hit by genocide, civil war, and the HIV/AIDS epidemic. Examples include Rwanda, with an extremely low life expectancy of 29 in 1994, the year of the Rwandan genocide, and Sierra Leone, with a life expectancy that did not surpass 40 until the year 2002, when the country's civil war ended. Zambia and Malawi have also had extremely low life expectances—below 50 for most of the period—due to the HIV/AIDS crisis. The relatively low life expectancy in sub-Saharan Africa corresponds with the region's relatively low real per capita GDP, which averaged $1,754 during the period. This average is considerably less than that of South and Southeast Asia ($3,881), Latin America and the Caribbean ($6,979), and Eastern Europe and Central Asia ($7,189).[4]

Sub-Saharan African countries also have lower rates of contraceptive usage than other countries. On average in sub-Saharan Africa, just 18% of married or in-union women of reproductive age reported that they used a modern contraceptive method, compared to at least 42% in the other regions. Benin, Guinea, Sierra Leone, and Mali had particularly low usage rates (7% or less) for most of the period. The region comprising Latin America and the Caribbean has the highest usage (54%) of modern contraceptive methods, with some of the highest rates found in Brazil, Colombia, and the Dominican Republic.

Although sub-Saharan Africa has the lowest average life expectancy and modern contraceptive usage in the region, it does not have the lowest abortion law index. Table A6.2 shows that the region comprising Latin America and the Caribbean has the lowest ranking for the average number of legal grounds upon which abortion is allowed. In fact, during this period four of the countries in the Latin American sample (Dominican Republic, Guatemala, Honduras, and Nicaragua) allowed abortion only on the grounds of saving the life of the woman. Nicaragua actually removed this allowance in 2007, so that abortion was completely prohibited. The only other sample country to criminalize all abortions during the period of analysis was Timor Leste.[5] At the other extreme, the highest average abortion law index is found in Eastern Europe and Central Asia, where the average country permits abortions on four legal grounds (typically, but not always, to save a woman's life, safeguard her physical health, protect her mental health, and when pregnancy is the result of rape or incest). Interestingly, of the 12 countries in this region, nine permit abortions on all the legal grounds. The exceptions are Egypt, Jordan, and Morocco, each of which is substantially more restrictive in its abortion policies. The final control variable, total non-US per capita financial assistance for family-planning and reproductive health services, also varies considerably across regions, with the highest average value of non-US per capita assistance going to sub-Saharan Africa. This value exceeds that of Eastern Europe and Central Asia, the lowest-ranking region, by more than a factor of five.

Table A6.2 also reports sample means by region for the dependent variable (whether or not the woman had an abortion) and the key independent variable (whether or not the woman lives in a high-exposure country). Consistent with the conclusions drawn earlier from the individual-country numbers in Table A6.1, women in Eastern Europe and Central Asia were more likely than women in other regions to have had an induced abortion during the period, with women in sub-Saharan Africa the least likely. Also of note, Latin America and the Caribbean stand out for having the lowest percentage of women (26.3%) living in high-exposure countries, which is about half that of the next lowest region. This relatively low rate reflects the DHS sample composition and the fact that the countries with the largest samples (Colombia, Dominican Republic, and Peru) are each low-exposure countries.

METHODOLOGY

The methodology tests whether the reinstatement of the global gag rule by President George W. Bush in 2001 is associated with a change in induced abortion rates in countries that had relatively high exposure to the US policy compared to countries with relatively low exposure and compared to before the policy was reinstated. A country's exposure to the policy is determined by its relative dependence on US assistance for family planning and reproductive health compared to other developing countries. The period of analysis is 1994 to 2008, with 1994–2000 considered the "before" period and 2001–2008 considered the "after" period, and the analysis examines women between the ages of 15 and 44.

The empirical analysis is based on a logistic regression that relates the odds of having an induced abortion to a measure of the global gag rule as well as a set of individual and country characteristics. The determinants of having an induced abortion are expressed as follows:

$$A_{ist} = a + \beta_1 PolEff_t + \beta_2 HiExp_s + \beta_3 PolEff_t * HiExp_s + \beta_4 X_{ist} + \vartheta_{ist},$$
(6.1)

where the subscript i denotes a woman, s denotes a country, and t denotes time. The dependent variable A_{ist} represents whether or not a woman i in country s and year t has an induced abortion. The notation $PolEff_t$ is a dummy variable for the years in which the global gag rule is in effect (so that it equals 0 for the years 1994–2000 and it equals 1 for the years 2001–2008). $HiExp_s$ is a dummy variable for countries with high exposure to the global gag rule (so that it equals 0 for countries with below-average aid flows from the United States, and it equals 1 for countries with above-average aid flows from the United States). The interaction between these two variables, $PolEff_t * HiExp_s$ is the key variable of interest, and when it equals 1, it identifies the combined effect of living in a high-exposure country in the years when the global gag rule was in effect. The notation X_{ist} is a set of individual and country characteristics that influence abortion decisions. The individual characteristics include the woman's age, educational attainment, marital status, and whether or not she lives in an urban area. The country-level characteristics include life expectancy, the rate of modern contraceptive usage, an index for national abortion laws, and the level of total official development assistance for family planning and reproductive health from all donors except the United States. Finally, ϑ_{ist} is an individual-specific idiosyncratic error term.

All regressions contain time-invariant, country-specific dummy variables that are common to all women in each country, as well as country-invariant, year-specific dummy variables that are common to all women in each year. The country fixed effects control for unobservable factors that influence a particular country's incidence of abortions but do not vary over time. For example, more egalitarian countries may be more likely to attract US foreign assistance and also have higher abortion rates. The year fixed effects control for other unobservable factors that may influence abortion rates, may change contemporaneously from year to year, and are common across countries. For example, if abortion rates trended upward over time due to the availability of safer methods across regions, this upward trend would be captured by the year fixed effects. More comprehensive information about the estimation procedure is found in the technical appendix to this chapter.

The estimation is performed separately for each of the four regions. The main reason for taking this approach is to examine how the effect of living in a high-exposure country after the reinstatement of the global gag rule differs across regions. Moreover, there is no reason to expect that the association between abortion rates and the control variables is the same across regions. That is, constraining the regression coefficients on all the independent variables to be the same across regions will most likely lead to misleading results given that each region differs in many ways with respect to societal norms, religions, legal structures, traditions, institutions, and so forth.

REGRESSION RESULTS

The full data set was used to estimate a logistic regression model that relates a woman's decision to have an induced abortion to her country's exposure to the global gag rule. The regression results, found in Table A6.3, are presented as odds ratios, with standard errors in parentheses. A detailed discussion of how to interpret an odds ratio is provided in the technical appendix, but as a rule of thumb, the odds ratio allows the researcher to determine how the likelihood of an event changes as a particular variable or condition changes. When the odds ratio equals 1, then the likelihood of the event occurring does not change. When the odds ratio is greater than 1, then the likelihood of the event happening increases, and when the odds ratio is less than 1, then the likelihood of the event happening decreases. Odds ratios are always positive numbers. So for any of the variables shown in Table A6.3, if the odds ratio equals 1, then the likelihood of a woman having an induced abortion does not change as a result of a change in that variable. When the odds ratio is greater than 1, a woman is more likely to have an induced abortion as a result of a change in that particular variable, and when the odds ratio is less than 1, a woman's likelihood of getting an induced abortion is reduced.

To be confident that the effects are systematic and not due to random chance, the result needs to be statistically significant, which in the table is indicated by asterisks next to the odds ratios. The notation *** indicates that the probability of the result occurring by random chance is less than 1%, ** indicates less than 5%, and * indicates less than 10%. Note that the results in Table A6.3 are presented separately for each of the four regions. For each region, the table reports three models: the first model includes only the measure of the global gag rule, the second adds the women's individual characteristics, and the third adds both the individual and the country characteristics. All three models include the country and year fixed effects.

Some of the strongest effects of the global gag rule among the four regions are found in Latin America and the Caribbean, the first region presented in Table A6.3. Results across Models 1 to 3 show a steady increase in the interaction effect for living in a high-exposure country while the policy was in place. In the basic model (Model 1), the result for the interaction term indicates that women in highly exposed countries in Latin America and the Caribbean had 1.60 times the odds of having an induced abortion after the reinstatement of the policy compared to before the policy and compared to women in less-exposed countries. This effect increases slightly to 1.71 in the model that adds controls for women's characteristics, and in the full model (Model 3), the odds ratio for the interaction term is 3.29. One can interpret this result as women in highly exposed countries having more than three times the odds of getting an abortion while the global gag rule was in effect compared to when it was not in effect and compared to women in less exposed countries. A likely explanation for this result is that women in the region had insufficient access to reproductive healthcare facilities as a result of the global gag rule, thus increasing unintended pregnancies and abortion rates. This interaction effect for the global gag rule is considerably larger than it is in the other regions, implying that all else equal, the US funding restrictions affected women's decision-making about abortion more in Latin America and the Caribbean than anywhere else.

The large change in the odds ratio across the models for Latin America and the Caribbean implies that the individual-level and especially the country-level characteristics play an important role in explaining variations in abortion rates across countries. Examining first the women's individual characteristics, it is clear that all four measures play a statistically significant and substantively meaningful role in explaining women's abortion decisions in the region. Women who have formal schooling have greater odds (by a factor of 1.33) of getting an induced abortion compared to their counterparts who do not have formal schooling. Similarly, women who live in urban areas have greater odds (by a factor of 1.52) of getting an induced abortion compared to women in rural areas. In the opposite direction, women who were never married have far lower odds (by a factor of 0.29) of getting an induced abortion compared to women who are married now or have been married in the past. As for women's age, the odds ratio of 0.97 implies that with each additional year of age, a woman's likelihood of getting an abortion is virtually the same as the year before.

Looking more closely at the full set of results in Model 3 for Latin America and the Caribbean, a country's life expectancy is not a statistically significant predictor of abortion rates. In contrast, a country's modern contraceptive usage, abortion law index, and total family-planning and reproductive health assistance from all other OECD countries are each statistically significant and substantively important. In particular, the 0.89 result for contraceptives indicates that when a country's usage of modern contraceptive methods rises by one percentage point, the relative odds of a woman having an induced abortion decrease. This result makes intuitive sense if one presumes that the use of modern contraceptives effectively helps to reduce unintended pregnancies and the need to seek an abortion. Moreover, an odds ratio for 0.92 for the abortion law index indicates that increasing the abortion law index by a value of 1 (which corresponds with increasing by 1 the legal grounds upon which a woman may obtain an abortion) actually reduces the relative odds of a woman having an induced abortion. The same conclusion applies in the reverse direction: reducing the abortion law index by a value of 1 (which corresponds with removing by 1 the legal grounds upon which women can get an abortion) will increase the relative odds of a woman seeking to have an abortion. Hence more restrictive abortion laws are associated with higher rates of induced abortion in Latin America and the Caribbean.

Interestingly, the odds ratio of 0.54 for a country's total non-US financial assistance per capita for family planning and reproductive health means that if this aid were to increase by $1 per person in an average Latin American country, the odds of women having an induced abortion would fall by about half. Combined with the finding for the measure of the global gag rule, this result suggests that women's abortion decisions are quite sensitive to the availability of facilities funded by foreign assistance. When US funds are restricted by the global gag rule, abortion rates rise substantially, and when other governments provide more money for family-planning and reproductive health services, abortion rates fall.

Results for Eastern Europe and Central Asia differ substantially from those of Latin America and the Caribbean. Notably, the interaction term is substantially below 1 (0.51 to 0.60 depending on the model) and it is statistically significant. The interpretation of this result is that women in highly exposed countries had about half the odds of getting an abortion after the reinstatement of the global gag rule compared to before the policy and compared to women in less exposed countries. The global gag rule thus appears to have reduced the availability of abortion services in this region, which was relatively high compared to other regions before the policy went into effect. Countering this effect, though, is a large increase in the odds of having an abortion (1.96) as the level of total non-US family-planning and reproductive health assistance rises: an increase of $1 in non-US foreign aid per capita almost doubles the odds of a woman having an induced abortion. Hence the reduction in abortion rates associated with the US funding cuts is completely offset by the increase in abortion rates associated with non-US financial assistance for family-planning and reproductive health services.

Pertaining to the other control variables, the odds ratio estimates for women's characteristics are comparable to those of Latin America and the Caribbean: the odds of getting an abortion are higher for women with formal schooling than for women without schooling; the odds of having an abortion are considerably lower for women who have never been married than for women who are currently or have been married; and the odds of having an abortion remain roughly the same with each year of age. The main difference between the two regions in the effects of women's characteristics is that living in an urban area no longer has a statistically significant association with abortion decisions. Countries in Eastern Europe and Central Asia also differ from those in Latin America and the

Caribbean when it comes to the association between some of the other country-level indicators and abortion decisions. In this case there is no statistically significant relationship between modern contraceptive prevalence and abortion, while adding additional legal grounds upon which women may obtain an abortion does increase the relative odds of women actually getting an abortion by a factor of 1.57 for each single increase in the permissible grounds for abortion.

The second half of Table A6.3 reports the regression results for South and Southeast Asia and for sub-Saharan Africa. The key result for the effect of the global gag rule in Asia is similar to that of Eastern Europe and Central Asia: namely, an odds ratio of 0.24 for the interaction effect in the full model implies that women in highly exposed countries had about one-quarter the odds of getting an abortion after the global gag rule was put back into place compared to before the policy and compared to women in less exposed countries. This result suggests that the global gag rule did work to reduce women's access to abortion services. Regarding the other indicators for women's characteristics, the results are similar to either or both of the regions just discussed: women with formal schooling and women in urban areas have considerably higher odds than their respective counterparts of getting an induced abortion, while women who were never married are much less likely to have an abortion. Interestingly, none of the country-level control variables are statistically significant.

In sub-Saharan Africa, the result for the key interaction term is similar to that of Latin America and the Caribbean, but smaller in magnitude. That is, an odds ratio of 2.08 for the interaction term in Model 3 indicates that women in highly exposed countries had more than double the odds of getting an induced abortion after the reinstatement of the policy compared to before the policy and compared to women in less exposed countries. This result is consistent with the argument that the global gag rule restricted women's access to family-planning and reproductive health services, thus contributing to unmet needs for contraception and a higher incidence of abortion. The estimate is slightly smaller but still comparable to the estimate of 2.55 for sub-Saharan Africa in Bendavid et al. (2011). The main reasons for the difference are the subsequent updates to the earlier DHS data sets for the sample countries, the addition of new waves of the DHS, and some small changes to the estimation procedure.

As with the results for Asia, none of the country-level characteristics have a statistically significant association with abortion rates in sub-Saharan Africa. The variables for women's characteristics do, however, appear to matter in influencing abortion decisions. Similar to the other regions, the likelihood of seeking an abortion does not change with an additional year of age. Also, women with formal schooling have more than double the odds of getting an abortion compared to women with no schooling, and women in urban areas also have higher odds of getting an abortion than their rural counterparts. In the opposite direction, never-married women have about half the odds of getting an abortion compared to their married counterparts.

CONCLUSION

This chapter has used logistic regression analysis to estimate the effect of the global gag rule on abortion rates across developing regions. The analysis was conducted with a very large data set of approximately 6.3 million women in 51 countries between the years 1994 and 2008. The key identification strategy of the regressions centered on a "difference in difference" approach that calculates the difference in abortion rates in countries with high and low exposure to the global gag rule, and how that difference compares before and after the 2001 reinstatement of the global gag rule.

Interestingly, the reinstatement of the global gag rule is associated with different responses in abortion rates across developing regions. In Latin America and the Caribbean and in sub-Saharan Africa, women in highly exposed countries had at least two times the odds of having an abortion after the reinstatement of the global gag rule compared to before the gag rule was put into place and compared to women in less exposed countries. This association between the gag rule and abortion rates was particularly large in Latin America and the Caribbean, where results from the full model with a complete set of individual- and country-level control variables indicate that women in countries with high exposure to the policy had more than three times the odds of having an abortion after the policy was in effect compared to women in countries with less exposure and before the policy was in effect. In contrast, the global gag rule worked in the opposite direction for women living in Eastern Europe and Central Asia, and for women in South and Southeast Asia. In these regions, the global gag rule is associated with lower odds of women having an induced abortion. However, in Eastern Europe and Central Asia, the lower odds of women seeking an abortion in high-exposure countries after the global gag rule was reinstated are counterbalanced by the increased odds of getting an abortion associated with financial assistance from other donor countries.

On net then, if the intent of the global gag rule was to discourage women from getting an abortion in the developing world, this policy failed to achieve its objective in the large majority of countries. The US policy is associated with a substantial increase in the likelihood of women having an abortion in sub-Saharan Africa and especially in Latin America and the Caribbean, and the negative effect of the US policy on abortion rates in Eastern Europe and Central Asia is completely offset by the positive effect of financial assistance from other donor countries. Only in South and Southeast Asia is the global gag rule associated with a reduction in the likelihood of women having an induced abortion that is not counteracted by other economy-wide forces. The reduction in abortions is presumably caused by clinic closures due to US funding cuts and fewer health professionals who are willing or able to provide abortions. That said, the region comprising South and Southeast Asia has some of the world's most densely populated countries, with pockets of extreme poverty, growing rates of HIV infection, and deeply entrenched biases against gender equality. Proponents of the US policy need to seriously consider whether women in these countries can afford to see reduced access to comprehensive reproductive healthcare services when the US restricts its financial assistance.

The analysis uncovered some strong similarities across developing regions when it comes to other determinants of women's abortion decisions. Consistently, women with formal schooling and women living in urban areas have greater odds of getting an induced abortion than their counterparts with no formal schooling and those living in rural areas. Another common pattern is that never-married women have considerably lower odds of having an induced abortion than women who are currently married or have been married in the past. However, the results point to fewer consistent patterns across regions when it comes to the importance of country-level characteristics in explaining abortion rates. The prevalence of modern contraceptives has a statistically significant association with abortion rates in just one region: Latin America and the Caribbean. As expected, higher usage rates of modern contraception are associated with lower abortion rates. This region also stands out for its relatively restrictive abortion laws. Ironically, the regression results suggest that the restrictiveness of the region's laws has done nothing to reduce abortion rates. More generally, across the four regions there is no definitive relationship between stricter abortion laws and women's likelihood of having an abortion. In one region stricter laws are associated with a greater likelihood of women having an abortion, in another region stricter laws reduce the likelihood of women seeking an abortion, and in the other two regions the association is not statistically significant. Legislative efforts and financial resources may be better spent on enhancing the quality and supply of reproductive healthcare services rather than trying to restrict access and institute laws that have unintended consequences.

TECHNICAL APPENDIX

The study estimates a fixed-effects logistic regression, which is a nonlinear regression model, that conditions out country-level and year-level heterogeneity. Each estimated coefficient (β) for a particular independent variable (X) in a logistic regression represents the change in the natural logarithm of the relative odds of the dependent variable associated with a one-unit change in the variable X. That is, $\beta = \ln(\text{relative odds})$, where odds are defined as a ratio of probabilities $p \,/\, (1 - p)$. Hence, the coefficients communicate direction of association—for example, which group of women have higher $(\beta > 0)$ or lower $(\beta < 0)$ chances of having an induced abortion. Note that the coefficients from a logistic regression capture the size of the association only relative to one another. Although the researcher can assess which factors have larger or smaller effects on the dependent variable, the size is not interpretable in an intuitively meaningful way. As a consequence, the effect estimates from a logistic regression are conventionally expressed in terms of odds ratios for each independent variable, which are easily interpretable in multiples or percentage changes in the odds of the outcome (UCLA, 2017; Long and Freese, 2014). The odds ratio for a particular variable is calculated by taking the exponential of the coefficient (odds ratio = e^{β}). For example, in a logistic regression of whether or not a woman has an induced abortion, an odds ratio of 2.0 for the variable "lives in urban area" is interpreted as follows: urban residents have twice the odds of having an induced abortion compared to their rural counterparts.

The odds ratios are computed using the logit command in Stata and the following coding:

xi: logit abort PolEff##HiExp i.country i.year, or cluster(country)

In this baseline regression (which does not include the additional control variables for individual and country characteristics), the command "xi" tells Stata to expand the variables for year and country into a set of dummy variables for individual years and countries (the country and year fixed effects). The command "logit" tells Stata to run a logistic regression, and the dependent variable is coded as "abort" (a dummy variable for whether or not a woman had an induced abortion in a particular year). The notation "PolEff##HiExp" signals to Stata what the first three independent variables are: a dummy variable for the years in which the global gag rule is in effect (2001–2008), a dummy variable for countries with high exposure to the global gag rule, and the interaction term in which these two variables are multiplied together. After the country and year fixed effects, the notation "or" tells Stata to report the odds ratios, and the notation "cluster(country)" tells Stata to cluster the standard errors by country. Standard errors are clustered by country to reduce potential bias that results from serial correlation in the independent variables. The cluster command produces the same coefficients as running a regression without the cluster option, but it yields different standard errors that account for arbitrary correlations within each country.

This first line of code generates the results presented in Table A6.3 in the columns for Model 1. The columns for Model 2 report results generated by the same line of code plus the four variables for women's characteristics. Similarly, the columns for Model 3 report results that add in not only the women's characteristics but also the four variables for country characteristics. To see how the effect of the global gag rule differs across developing regions, these models are estimated separately for each of the four regions. Hence Table A6.3 presents a series of odds ratios from 12 separate logistic regressions (3 models times 4 regions).

Note that the terms "logistic" and "logit" are often used interchangeably in the literature. Technically, a logistic regression estimates a maximum likelihood logit model. The logit model is linear in terms of the natural log of the odds (the logit), but nonlinear in the metric of probabilities. In particular, a predicted probability from the model varies as the value of an independent variable changes, and it depends on the values of all the variables in the model (UCLA, 2017; Long and Freese, 2014). Interaction terms, the standard "difference in difference" estimators in most models, are notoriously difficult to interpret in nonlinear models. With logistic regressions, the difference-in-difference results can be presented in terms of log odds (the β coefficients), odds ratios (e^{β}), or probability (p). The fact that these metrics can yield different conclusions adds to the difficulty in modeling and interpreting interaction effects. This chapter uses the odds ratio metric because the interaction effects are easier to interpret than log odds, and the computation for the interaction effect remains the same regardless of the values assigned to the other control variables.

The results for each independent variable in Table A6.3 are thus odds ratios, and the result for each interaction effect is a ratio of odds ratios, which means that the difference-in-difference effect is multiplicative in nature rather than additive, as it would be in other models or estimation procedures. Specifically, the reported result for each interaction term in Table A6.3 is interpreted as the ratio of two odds ratios (OR) as follows:

$$\text{Interaction effect} = \frac{Odds\left(HiExp=1, PolEff=1\right)/Odds\left(HiExp=0, PolEff=1\right)}{Odds\left(HiExp=1, PolEff=0\right)/Odds\left(HiExp=0, PolEff=0\right)}$$

Intuitively, the result for the interaction term compares the effect on abortion rates after the policy was reinstated in high-exposure countries and low-exposure countries, relative to the effect on abortion rates before the policy was reinstated in high-exposure and low-exposure countries. So, for example, if $Odds(HiExp=1, PolEff=1)/Odds(HiExp=0, PolEff=1)$ equals 3, this means that the odds of women having an abortion are 3 times greater for high-exposure countries than low-exposure countries while the policy was in effect. Moreover, if $Odds(HiExp=1, PolEff=0)/Odds(HiExp=0, PolEff=0)$ equals 2, this means that the odds of women having an abortion are 2 times greater for high-exposure countries than low-exposure countries before the policy was in effect. The overall interaction effect is 3 / 2 = 1.5, so women in highly exposed countries had 1.5 times the odds of having an abortion after the reinstatement of the policy compared to before the policy and compared to women in less exposed countries.

NOTES

1. As shown in Table A6.1, the regional category "Eastern Europe and Central Asia" includes countries from several regions in the greater area: Eastern Europe, Central Asia, West Asia, the Middle East, and North Africa. For ease of exposition, I chose "Eastern Europe and Central Asia" as the label.
2. Adjustments needed to be made to the year and the century month code (cmc) entries in the DHS data for Ethiopia and Nepal because these countries do not use the Gregorian calendar.
3. Sample means in Table A6.2 are weighted using the DHS sampling weights.
4. These averages are constructed using World Bank (2017) data on real GDP per capita (in 2011 purchasing-power-parity-converted international US$) for each of the sample countries. Regression results were very similar when real GDP per capita was added to the regressions as a control variable instead of life expectancy.
5. Timor Leste was also the only sample country for which the UNDESA (2015b) source had incomplete data. The information on Timor Leste's criminalization of all abortions is from Belton, Whittaker, Fonseca, Wells-Brown, and Pais (2009).

Conclusion

This book's systematic analysis yields three important messages about the global gag rule and other policy restrictions on women's reproductive health. First, in the majority of countries that receive US family-planning assistance, the global gag rule has failed to achieve its goal of reducing abortions. Econometric results in the previous chapter suggest that overall, the 2017 reinstatement of the global gag rule is likely to result in more, not fewer, abortions globally. The findings indicate that the odds of women getting an abortion increased by a factor of three in Latin America and the Caribbean and a factor of two in sub-Saharan Africa as result of the global gag rule when it was in effect from 2001 to 2008. While the global gag rule reduced the likelihood of getting an abortion in Eastern Europe and Central Asia, this decline was completely offset by the effect of financial assistance from other countries. Only in South and Southeast Asia did the global gag rule appear to restrict women's access to abortion. However, with its pockets of high population density, gender inequality, and growing rates of HIV infection, this region cannot afford to see disruptions to comprehensive reproductive health services that come with US restrictions on family-planning assistance.

Second, there is no definitive relationship between restrictive national abortion laws and women's likelihood of having an abortion. Rather, restrictive legislation is associated with more unsafe abortions. Abortion is completely banned or only permitted to save a woman's life in 66 countries, accounting for roughly one-quarter of the world's population. Yet despite the legal prohibitions and restrictions, abortion remains common across developing countries, and a substantial percentage of maternal mortality is attributed to unsafe abortions. No study has found evidence that restricting women's access to abortion has a measurable impact on reducing abortion rates, just as the econometric estimates in Chapter 6 find no systematic relationship between the restrictiveness of abortion legislation and the odds of women seeking an abortion. If anything, countries with restrictive national legislation have higher rates of unsafe abortion, more need for postabortion care, and greater maternal mortality. Women living in countries with restrictive national laws face a double blow to their reproductive health whenever the global gag rule is reinstated: they have fewer options to access contraceptive methods and even fewer options to access safe abortions.

Third, the 2017 reinstatement of the global gag rule will have negative repercussions for a range of health outcomes for women, men, and children in developing countries. The weight of the evidence indicates that family-planning programs have beneficial effects for reducing fertility and improving women's and children's health. Thus, disrupting these programs is likely to have adverse effects for women and children. Given the expansion of the policy from family-planning assistance to all global health funding, the 2017 global gag rule is expected to have additional impacts for individuals who may not have been impacted by the restrictions on family planning alone. The book closes with an alternative plan that can improve the effectiveness of US financial assistance for family planning and reproductive health. The United States has a long history of providing assistance for family planning and playing a leading role in advocating for women's reproductive health. An alternative plan that targets integrated reproductive health services will have more success than the global gag rule in achieving the goals that the United States has a history of supporting.

GLOBAL GAG RULE FAILS TO ACHIEVE ITS GOAL OF REDUCING ABORTIONS

The econometric estimates in the previous chapter point to considerable differences across regions in the impact of the 2001 reinstatement of the global gag rule, with the policy leading to higher abortion rates in two regions that have the most restrictive abortion laws. In particular, the odds of women getting an abortion rose by a factor of three in Latin America and the Caribbean and a factor of two in sub-Saharan Africa. The most likely mechanism for this substantial increase in the odds of getting an abortion is that the global gag rule caused major disruptions to family-planning services, which reduced access to contraception, led to more unintended pregnancies, and contributed to higher abortion rates. On the other hand, the odds of getting an abortion dropped in South and Southeast Asia and in Eastern Europe and Central Asia. In the latter region, this decline was completely offset by other forces, especially greater funding from other donors.

What might explain some of the regional differences? In the context of the theoretical model presented in Chapter 4, recall that funding restrictions due to the global gag rule cause an increase in the cost of purchasing and accessing contraceptive methods, which is represented as an upward shift in the marginal cost of contraceptive intensity. When the cost of giving birth is less than the cost of having an abortion, women choose the level of contraceptive intensity where the marginal cost of contraception equals the cost of giving birth, which in the new equilibrium is now at a lower level of contraceptive intensity and a lower likelihood of preventing pregnancy. In the event of unintended pregnancies, women will tend to give birth rather than have an abortion. This scenario would help to explain the empirical results for South and Southeast Asia as well as Eastern Europe and Central Asia. When the cost of having an abortion is less than the cost of giving birth, women choose the level of contraceptive intensity where the marginal cost of contraception equals the cost of having an abortion, which again is at a lower level of contraceptive intensity and a lower likelihood of preventing pregnancy. In the event of unintended pregnancies, women will tend to have an abortion rather than carry the pregnancy to term. This scenario would help to explain the empirical results for Latin America and the Caribbean as well as sub-Saharan Africa.

Why might the line representing the cost of abortion fell below the line representing the cost of giving birth? Unfortunately there are no available data comparing the monetary costs of having an abortion or giving birth across countries, so we are left to turn to other variables that would affect these overall costs. One such variable is the overall normative climate around abortion within a country, with the reasoning that the total cost of getting an abortion, including the emotional cost, is lower in countries where the normative climate around abortion is more accepting. Given the estimates of high abortion rates in countries with restrictive national legislation, it is likely that the overall normative environment matters even more than a country's national abortion laws in determining women's decisions about abortion.

The overall normative environment, in turn, is related to the predominant religion in a country as well as individual attitudes toward abortion. A good source of information on religion and attitudes toward abortion is the World Values Survey, a set of surveys done every five years on people's beliefs and values in about 100 countries.[1] One of the questions asked of respondents is when abortion can be justified, with responses ranging from 1 (never) to 10 (always). The survey also asks if respondents belong to a certain religion and if so, which one. To better understand the potential links between religion and attitudes toward abortion, the World Values Survey for 2010–2014 (the most recent available) was used examine the percentage of a country's population that declares itself to belong to a certain religion and how that percentage is correlated with the percentage of a country's population that says that abortion can never be justified. The data for constructing these variables are reported in Table A7.1, and the correlation coefficients are found in Table A7.2. The strongest positive correlation (.45) between religion and the percentage of the population who believes that abortion is never justified is for people who are Muslim. The greater the percentage of a population that is Muslim, the higher the percentage of people who believe that abortion is never justified. A similar result holds for the percentage of a population that is Protestant, Hindu, or Buddhist. In the opposite direction, people who have no religion are less likely to believe that abortion is never justified, with a correlation coefficient of –.62. Somewhat surprisingly, there is also a negative correlation, albeit quite weak, between the percentage of a population that identifies as being Roman Catholic and the percentage who believe that abortion is never justified. Even though the Catholic Church has historically acted as one of the strongest forces against abortion in global politics and debates, individuals of Catholic faith seem to be more tolerant of abortion. The category "other religions" and the Orthodox Church also have a negative correlation coefficient.

These conclusions about the correlation between religion and tolerance of abortion also apply when attitudes toward abortion are measured as the average score in a country for the extent to which a person believes abortion can be justified. An average score of 1 indicates that abortion cannot be justified at all, and an average score of 10 indicates that abortion can be completely justified. As shown in the second column of Table A7.2, the greater the percentage of a population that is Muslim, Protestant, Hindu, or Buddhist, the lower the average tolerance toward abortion. The opposite holds for Roman Catholic, Orthodox, other religions, and no religion.

Also informative is to see how attitudes toward abortion have changed over time. Table A7.3 reports this information using the same World Values Survey data. All countries with available data on attitudes toward abortion in both 1995–1999 and 2010–2014 are categorized according to the predominant religion, defined as the religion within each country accounting for the highest percentage of the population. The table indicates that the majority of predominantly Catholic countries in the sample became more tolerant toward abortion between these two time periods, with proportionately fewer people saying that they could never justify abortion. Also, the average score for the degree to which abortion could be justified rose over time for the majority of predominantly Catholic countries. In the opposite direction, countries that are predominantly Orthodox all became less tolerant of abortion over time, with proportionately more people reporting that abortion is never justified and people reporting a lower mean score for the extent to which they can justify abortion. Similarly, two of the three predominantly Muslim countries became less tolerant of abortion over time. For the other categories, it is harder to make a conclusion about changes in tolerance over time either because there are too few countries in the religion categories or there were no clear patterns among the countries within a category.

These results could help to explain why restrictions on family-planning assistance due to the global gag rule are associated with the greatest increase in women's odds of getting an abortion in Latin America and the Caribbean, a region comprised of predominantly Catholic countries.

Not only are countries likely to show more tolerance of abortion as the proportion of people who identify as Catholic increases, but abortion tolerance appears to have increased over time. This conclusion is consistent with published evidence that despite the Catholic Church's strict stance against abortion and the restrictive abortion laws in most Latin American countries, some of the highest abortion rates globally are seen among Catholic women (Morgan and Roberts, 2012). It is harder to draw conclusions about religion and attitudes toward abortion for the other three major regions examined in the econometric analysis given their diversity of religions. For these regions, it would be helpful to know more about the total costs of giving birth relative to having an abortion and how these costs may be affected by the global gag rule. For example, if women in highly exposed countries are afraid that there will be insufficient healthcare for sick children after they give birth, they may opt to have an abortion instead. This would help to explain the higher odds of getting an abortion in sub-Saharan Africa, which as a region was highly exposed to the global gag rule.

RESTRICTIVE LEGISLATION ASSOCIATED WITH MORE UNSAFE ABORTIONS

There is no definitive relationship between stricter national abortion laws and women's likelihood of having an abortion. Widely cited research reviewed in Chapter 5 shows no association between abortion rates across countries and the legal status of abortion in those countries. If anything, countries with more legal restrictions actually have higher abortion rates, and many of those abortions are unsafe and result in complications and even death. Chapter 5's analysis of published data shows that unsafe abortion rates are more than four times higher in countries with restrictive abortion policies than in countries with liberal policies. Some of this differential reflects disparities in economic development between countries with restrictive versus liberal abortion policies, since countries with restrictive policies tend to be less developed and have inadequate healthcare infrastructure and services. However, it is difficult to dispute the argument that restrictive laws lead to fewer safe and reliable providers of abortion services, thus forcing women to resort to unsafe providers or self-induced abortion.

Latin America and the Caribbean and sub-Saharan Africa have the most restrictive abortion laws in the world, yet abortion rates (often illegal) are extremely high. This book's econometric work shows that the 2001–2008 iteration of the global gag rule resulted in greater odds of getting an abortion in these regions, with the implication that many of the additional abortions were performed under unsafe conditions that heightened women's risks of complications. This finding of the largest impact of the global gag rule in the two regions with the most restrictive abortion laws makes it very difficult to rationalize US restrictions on women's reproductive health that further prevent women from accessing safe abortion services.

The regression results in Chapter 6 also demonstrate that across the four regions analyzed, there is no definitive relationship between stricter abortion laws and women's likelihood of having an abortion. In one region (Latin America and the Caribbean) stricter laws are associated with a greater likelihood of women having an abortion; in another region (Eastern Europe and Central Asia) stricter laws are associated with a lower likelihood of women seeking an abortion; and in the other two regions (South and Southeast Asia, and sub-Saharan Africa) the association is not statistically significant. Women will find pathways to abortion if they need to despite the legal restrictions, and in countries where the climate is more accepting of abortion, those pathways may be easier to find. This argument is consistent with a comment made by Professor Catriona Macleod from Rhodes University in South Africa in a 2017 interview about the global gag rule:

> [Young people's] knowledge of legal abortion is very poor, but then you ask them about unsafe or illegal abortion and methods that they've heard about . . . and you find the most remarkable knowledge on how to self-perform abortion. . . . And yet, their legal rights are something they just don't know about. . . . So that's [unsafe abortion] going to be perpetuated now.[2]

The argument that women will find avenues toward abortion no matter what the legal environment is particularly relevant in countries where the "abortion pill" misoprostol has become more available through the internet, black market, and local pharmacies. The increased availability and affordability of misoprostol has made medical abortion a more feasible option for women seeking to terminate unintended pregnancies even in the face of legal restrictions.

A large number of developing countries still have abortion legislation that either prohibits abortion altogether or allows it only to save the life of the woman. Even when they are legally allowed, abortion services are often separated from other health services. This separation has only served to marginalize women who seek abortions and has made it more difficult to reduce the incidence of unsafe abortions. US funding restrictions implemented through the Helms Amendment and the global gag rule have only reinforced this long-standing marginalization of abortion from other healthcare services. Legislative efforts and financial resources may be better spent on enhancing the quality and supply of reproductive healthcare services rather than trying to restrict access and institute laws that have unintended consequences.

ADVERSE IMPACTS OF GAG RULE EXTEND ACROSS A DASHBOARD OF INDICATORS

The 2017 expanded version of the global gag rule is likely to have adverse effects—both direct and indirect—on a dashboard of health indicators for women, men, and children. The direct effects result from cuts in funding to programs that deliver vital health services. With interruptions to these services, individuals risk not receiving the preventive care and medical treatment that they need. The indirect impacts occur through higher fertility rates that are likely to result from reduced contraceptive access (Bingenheimer and Skuster, 2017). Just how large will these adverse impacts be? It is exceedingly difficult to come up with a plausible set of projections, not least because it is still too early to tell the extent of US funding cuts and how much other donors will step in to make up for the shortfall. Moreover, the composition of total funding may change again, similar to what happened beginning in the early 2000s with a large shift in priorities toward HIV/AIDS prevention and treatment. It is a complicated picture. Not only do we not know how much total funding will be cut or reallocated, we also do not know the extent to which other donors will step in, the degree to which providers may increase their fees, or the sensitivity of various health outcomes to fluctuations in funding.

Chapter 2 shows that when the global gag rule was reinstated in 2001, total US family-planning assistance dropped almost 50% the following year, from $312 million to $161 million. On net, the 2001 iteration of the global gag rule led to a 3% to 6% reduction in total family-planning assistance from all donor countries for the entire period the policy was in effect, and countries with high fertility rates were more susceptible to the cuts (Asiedu, Nanivazo, and Nkusu, 2013). Fast-forward to the 2017 gag rule: a 50% drop in family-planning assistance would amount to approximately $300 million, down from $612 million in 2016. However, a Dutch-led campaign (the "She Decides" fund) was launched soon after Trump's reinstatement of the global gag rule, and as of late 2017 this campaign had already raised over $300 million. Depending on how many years this campaign continues to offset the shortfall due to the US restrictions, it would not be unreasonable to use a 3% to 6% reduction in total family-planning assistance from all donor countries as an estimate for total funding cuts.

Of course these numbers pertain only to assistance for family planning and reproductive health, not to all global health funding. At the most extreme, if all global health funding were to be cut off (a total pot of about $10 billion), the United States would no longer contribute bilateral assistance for a number of vital programs, including HIV/AIDS prevention and treatment, maternal and child health, nutrition, global health security, and prevention and treatment of malaria, tuberculosis, and other tropical diseases. Recent data indicate that US funding accounts for 34% of total development assistance for health from all donor countries (IHME, 2017). Elimination of this support would deliver a major blow to important interventions that have saved millions of lives, including the President's Emergency Plan for AIDS Relief (PEPFAR) and the President's Malaria Initiative (PMI), both of which were introduced and expanded with bipartisan support.

In trying to project possible funding cuts, it is important to remember that the global gag rule targets foreign NGOs, and many choose to comply with the terms of the policy so their funding is not cut off. The most notable changes then are directed toward the end of abortion services if the NGOs were providing such services before the policy change. Only those NGOs that do not comply see a reduction in funding. Evidence in a 2017 Kaiser Family Foundation report indicates that an extreme termination of all global health funding is unlikely to happen (Moss and Kates, 2017). The report's projections, based on the preceding three years, indicate that at least 1,275 foreign NGOs and close to $2.2 billion in funding allocated to those NGOs could be subject to the terms of the 2017 expanded global gag rule. In addition, at least 469 US NGOs that received global health assistance from the government would have had to guarantee that their foreign partners were in compliance. If all those NGOs had decided to not comply with the policy, global health assistance from the United States would have fallen by over $2 billion, of which the largest portion is devoted to HIV/AIDS prevention and treatment. This is a substantial sum of money that is difficult for other donor countries to match.

It is an even bigger challenge to project the magnitude of the impacts that the funding cuts will have on actual health and well-being. What we can do is discuss the indicators of health and well-being that are most likely to change and in which direction. One of the direct effects and probably the biggest health concern associated with the global gag rule is that the funding restrictions will disrupt women's access to family planning, cause an increase in unintended pregnancies, and lead to more unsafe abortions. The evidence in Chapter 2 suggests that the reinstatement of the policy in 2001 by George W. Bush caused substantial disruptions to the provision of contraceptive services. This chapter shows that US family-planning assistance dropped sharply in 2002 and stayed low until 2007. The United States also terminated its annual contribution to the United Nations Population Fund beginning in 2001, which added to the financial restrictions on international organizations caused by the global gag rule.

As discussed in Chapter 2, the global gag rule impacted family-planning and reproductive health services through two major channels. Those organizations that chose not to comply with the terms of the US policy—including the International Planned Parenthood Federation and Marie Stopes International, the world's largest NGOs providing family-planning services—lost their financial support from USAID. These cuts contributed to extensive clinic closures, NGO staff reductions, and contraceptive supply shortages. Those organizations that chose to comply with the policy in order to retain their funding were forced to offer less comprehensive services that excluded abortion procedures, counseling, and referrals. Additional evidence in Chapter 3 demonstrates that after the United States started committing foreign aid to population assistance in 1965, it quickly became the dominant international source of financial assistance for family planning and reproductive health. Since that time, assistance from the United States has comprised over half of all population assistance from donor countries. The world's poorest countries, especially those in sub-Saharan Africa, are most dependent on funding from international donors and have been unable to offset the US shortfall with funds from other sources.

Increases in unintended pregnancies due to reduced contraceptive access in the face of highly restrictive national abortion laws are likely to result in more unsafe abortions. Between 2005 and 2012, even though the total abortion rate globally declined, the number of unsafe abortions actually increased: close to 7 million women in developing countries received treatment for abortion complications in 2012, up from 5 million in 2005 (Singh and Maddow-Zimet, 2016). Further estimates indicate that an additional 3 million women who had complications from unsafe abortions did not receive postabortion care (Singh and Maddow-Zimet, 2016). Could the 2017 reinstatement of the global gag rule impact millions of women, as some media sources predicted? The weight of the evidence supports this prediction. For example, Marie Stopes International (MSI)—just one of several large family-planning NGOs providing safe abortion services that chose not to comply with the terms of the global gag rule—estimates that 1.5 million women each year will lose access to MSI-provided contraceptive services due to its loss of USAID funding, which averaged $30 million annually in recent years. Between 2017 and 2020, the loss in MSI services is projected to lead to 2.2 million additional abortions (most of them unsafe) and 21,700 maternal deaths, as well as an increase in healthcare costs of $400 million (MSI, 2017).

Another direct effect of the funding cuts is reduced access to maternal and child health services and other reproductive health services.

As discussed in PAI (2005), the funding cuts from the 2001 reinstatement of the global gag rule affected not only family planning but also other health services that were offered through the affected clinics. These services included prenatal and antenatal obstetric care, infant and child healthcare, immunizations, cervical cancer screening, malaria treatment, and screening and treatment for sexually transmitted infections including HIV/AIDS. Unfortunately there is no empirical evidence showing the extent to which health outcomes were affected by the global gag rule under previous administrations, but it is difficult to dispute that women, children, and men would have been vulnerable to reduced access to these services. It is still too early to assess the impact of the 2017 expanded global gag rule, but initial research findings from Human Rights Watch released in October 2017—based on interviews in Kenya and Uganda—indicate substantial reductions in key reproductive and sexual health services, a great deal of confusion and fear about the policy implementation, and a weakening in coalitions fighting to end maternal mortality (HRW, 2017).

The extended gag rule can have additional effects, especially for men and women with HIV/AIDS, since all global health funding is at stake. As discussed in Chapter 2, HIV/AIDS prevention and treatment has comprised more than half of US global health assistance since 2006. Most of these funds have been channeled through PEPFAR, a program that as of 2017 has provided antiretroviral treatment to approximately 13.3 million people and also supported HIV testing and counseling for 85.5 million people (PEPFAR, 2017). PEPFAR is estimated to have averted 2.9 million HIV infections across 16 African countries receiving these funds within nine years after the program was launched (Heaton et al., 2015). Moreover, estimates in Bendavid and Battacharya (2009) indicate that the annual change in AIDS-related deaths in PEPFAR countries was 10.5% lower than in countries not receiving PEPFAR funds. To the extent that health providers using PEPFAR funds to provide these services choose to not comply with the terms of the global gag rule (that is, they choose to continue to provide health services that include abortion-related activities), then HIV infections and deaths due to AIDS will no longer be prevented at the same rate. Conversely, health providers that decide to comply with the policy will be forced to stop providing abortion services and counseling, which increases the risk of more births of HIV-infected children. These impacts from the global gag rule will go above and beyond adverse impacts caused by other funding cuts, such as Trump's $800 million cuts in funds for global HIV/AIDS prevention and treatment in the budget proposal for fiscal year 2018. These proposed cuts could have led to 200,000 additional HIV infections in one year alone (Gramer, 2017).

Funding for prevention and treatment of other diseases—including tuberculosis, the Ebola virus, and the Zika virus—is also at risk. Any NGO focusing on these diseases that also provides family-planning services and happens to even mention abortion could have its US funding terminated. This threat is particularly troubling in Latin America, which experienced a Zika virus epidemic in 2016. Because the disease was linked to severe brain malformations in babies born to women carrying the virus, many governments in the region issued unprecedented warnings for women to avoid pregnancy (Singh and Karim, 2017). Although the number of cases fell substantially in 2017, there is no drug to prevent or treat Zika, so women in the region still seeking to delay pregnancy are doing so in the face of funding cuts for family planning as a result of the global gag rule.

As a case in point, in 2016 the International Planned Parenthood Federation / Western Hemisphere Region (IPPF/WHR) received over $1 million in USAID money through a secondary partnership to work on the Zika virus. This funding came on top of another $1 million grant to fight HIV. The NGO expects to lose both grants in 2018 because it has refused to comply with the terms of the global gag rule. One official with IPPF/WHR said in an interview, "It's a small percentage of our budget, but it is money that is hard to come by because the region is not a priority."[3] A big reason that Latin America is no longer a priority for USAID is that most countries in the region are middle-income countries. However, as noted by this official, "The averages hide huge inequalities, where women experience the brunt of the challenges. . . . In the case of Brazil, most of the women that experience Zika with very difficult consequences are black or brown women, and they tend to be poor." This situation with Zika funding cuts is a prime example of how the global gag rule not only denies financial assistance to vulnerable populations, but does so in very racialized, classed, and gendered ways.

The global gag rule can have indirect health effects through increases in women's fertility. Chapter 4 highlights a large body of scholarship showing that family-planning programs in developing countries contribute to higher rates of contraceptive use and lower fertility rates. Although some scholars argue that the main force behind lower fertility is economic development, a number of studies find that family-planning programs help to lower fertility rates by reducing the obstacles that women face in using modern contraceptives. By backward reasoning then, disruptions to family-planning programs are likely to reduce contraceptive usage, which increases the risk of unintended pregnancies and higher fertility. Additional descriptive evidence in Chapter 4 points to a clear negative association between contraceptive prevalence and fertility, suggesting that if contraceptive prevalence declines as a result of funding cuts, fertility will rise. Moreover, estimates in Jones (2015) for Ghana indicate that the 2001 global gag rule resulted in an increase in fertility rates of anywhere from 3% to 11% depending on the demographic group.

Higher fertility is associated with shorter spacing between births and larger family size, both of which have adverse effects on children's nutritional status, development, and survival chances (Joshi and Schultz, 2013). Numerous studies on investments in children's human capital find that larger family size decreases resource availability per child, which is linked to worsened child health and lower educational attainment. For these reasons family-planning programs are positively associated with child health and well-being, and disruptions to these services through the global gag rule can have adverse effects on child health (Canning and Schultz, 2012).

It is not just children who are affected by changes in fertility rates, but also women themselves. Higher maternal age at first birth, fewer children, and longer birth intervals each result from women's ability to control the timing and number of births, and each has been linked to improved maternal health, higher body mass index, increased educational attainment, higher labor force participation rates, and increased lifetime earnings. These positive effects for women have been well documented in the literature.[4] Some of the effects, especially higher educational attainment, can even result from contraceptive access, not necessarily contraceptive use. For example, parents may have an incentive to invest more in their daughters' education if they know that their daughters will have access to contraception later in life and can delay their fertility (Babiarz, Lee, Miller, Peng, and Valente, 2017). The beneficial effects for women, in turn, may have feedback effects for their children's health in the future, as child health has been linked to various measures of health and economic empowerment of their mothers, especially maternal education. A review of studies of these various indirect effects of family planning programs on women's and children's health through the link of lower fertility indicates that the estimates tend to be modest in size but meaningful in practicality (Miller and Babiarz, 2016).

Another indirect effect of the global gag rule and cutbacks in family-planning services is stress on the environment. Population growth may play an even bigger role than climate change in contributing to environmental threats and degradation (Worldwatch Institute, 2016). There are several channels through which the global gag rule could impact the environment. The first is through population size; less funding for family planning could result in an increase in fertility, which would contribute to increased population growth, which in turn places more stress on the environment. The second channel is through women's empowerment. When women can control their fertility through family planning, they are empowered to participate in other activities beyond childcare, including civic affairs. Studies have shown that when women are included in decision-making groups that control natural resources, monitoring efforts lead to better environmental outcomes such as forest regeneration and protection of endangered species. For example, in India and Nepal, community forest organizations that had proportionately more women on their executive committees were able to maintain healthier forests as measured by biodiversity, canopy, and tree growth over time (Agarwal, 2009). A policy such as the global gag rule that reverses the benefits to women of lower fertility could hamper women's ability to contribute to environmental conservation (Worldwatch Institute, 2016).

A MORE CONSTRUCTIVE APPROACH FOR US FAMILY-PLANNING ASSISTANCE

Economists often conclude their studies with policy implications, and a clear implication of the analysis in this book is to replace the global gag rule with a more constructive approach for US foreign aid to target women's reproductive health in developing countries. The book has presented a wealth of evidence showing that the global gag rule—renamed by the Trump administration as "Protecting Life in Global Health Assistance"—does not achieve its objectives in the majority of countries that receive US assistance. This evidence helps to bolster arguments made by critics following the 2017 reinstatement that the policy is counterproductive and has unintended effects. One example of many such claims is a comment made in a 2017 interview by a service provider in Nigeria: "It is an unfair provision and it does directly the opposite of what it is intended to do. It denies life-saving services to a lot of women. It ends up being really anti-life."[5] In light of the evidence, the book closes with an alternative approach to protecting life that centers on integrated reproductive health services.

Integrating family planning and safe abortion into a full range of reproductive health services will go a long way to promoting health equity and reducing maternal morbidity and mortality. This strategy is consistent not only with international agreements such as the one made at the 1994 International Conference on Population and Development in Cairo, but also with recommendations made by scholars, major multilateral agencies such as the World Health Organization and World Bank, health professionals, and advocates. For example, Barbara Crane, a former official with the family-planning organization Ipas, made a strong case for integrated health services as the key for reducing unsafe abortions:

> We need stronger health systems and we need integrated service delivery. One of the problems is that family planning has often been kept separate from other health service delivery and verticalized, and abortion even more so. How do you break the cycle of unwanted pregnancy and unsafe abortion? You need to help women have access to services. . . . All it [the global gag rule] does is marginalize women who have a clear and desperate need for these services and makes it harder for them to get access, and it stigmatizes providers.[6]

This marginalization of women who seek family-planning and abortion services has made it more difficult to reduce unsafe abortion rates.

Unsafe abortion is a leading cause of maternal morbidity and mortality. Globally, about 300,000 deaths due to pregnancy and childbirth occur each year; about 8% to 15% of these maternal deaths are attributed to abortion (Say et al., 2014; Kassebaum et al., 2014). The statistics on unsafe abortions and maternal mortality are hard to accept, especially with the great strides in technological progress and with the knowledge and resources available in high-income economies. Still, a very high number of women die of causes that are preventable in nature. Adopting a broader strategy aimed at providing women with an integrated package of services for their reproductive health will constitute a big step toward reducing global inequities in maternal mortality. Given the emphasis that governments and donors have placed on reducing maternal mortality and improving women's reproductive health, it makes sense to focus on the entire continuum of women's reproductive health needs.

Maternal mortality remains a major concern in low-income countries where the lack of skilled health professionals during deliveries makes it difficult to treat obstetric complications such as hemorrhage, hypertension, and sepsis. Insufficient access to medical care around the time of delivery is a crucial reason why pregnancy and childbirth still result in high rates of maternal mortality in low-income countries. In emergency situations at birth the critical priority is to ensure timely support from skilled professionals. Inadequacies in appropriate medical facilities and trained staff are driven largely by insufficient spending on maternal health, which is considerably lower than other health sector interventions in most countries (WHO, 2015). More US foreign aid for maternal health, including the development of health infrastructure and the training of skilled health professionals, will help to address these inequities.

There is abundant evidence on various "best practices" in reproductive health services that warrant scaling up and replication in other developing countries. Widespread adoption of such policies and integrating them into a range of reproductive health services would help to bring meaningful changes to women's reproductive health. Two examples of many include Malawi's "Option B+" program, in which all HIV-positive women who were pregnant and breastfeeding became eligible for lifelong antiretroviral treatment, and the Rwandan government's commitment to investing in the supply chain for contraceptives and making all family-planning services and products free of charge (PAI, 2015). Greater US support for endeavors like these would make US foreign aid policy more beneficial in promoting women's reproductive health and rights in developing countries.

Not only would prioritizing a broad range of reproductive healthcare services better meet women's health needs, it would also be more cost effective than current strategies of marginalizing and restricting family-planning and abortion services. The main repercussion of the legal and financial restrictions is to change the conditions under which women obtain abortions, thus intensifying the problem of unsafe abortion. Postabortion care, which is supported by US foreign aid, has become the de facto solution to the problem of unsafe abortions. Postabortion care is essentially a two-step process of first saving a woman's life after she has an unsafe abortion and then providing her with modern contraception to prevent the cycle from happening again. The total cost of postabortion care to public health systems in developing countries is high, and governments would save money by refocusing their efforts on providing women with more access to modern contraception. Estimates in Vlassoff, Singh, and Onda (2016) for a sample of developing countries indicate that the total cost of postabortion care per case ranges from $334 in Rwanda to $972 in Colombia, which constitutes up to 35% of annual per capita income depending on the country. The authors estimate that the cost of meeting a woman's unmet need for modern contraceptive supplies and services for one year would amount to just 3% to 12% of the average cost of treating a patient who requires postabortion care. A more proactive US foreign aid policy would, true to the policy's new focus on "protecting life," protect women's lives by supporting this approach in a continuum of reproductive health services.

The total cost of fully meeting the needs of women and newborns for a complete package of reproductive health services—including full coverage of modern contraception, maternal and newborn healthcare, safe abortion services, postabortion care, treatment for sexually transmitted infections, and HIV testing of pregnant women and antiretroviral treatment of those living with HIV—would be about $53.6 billion every year. This total is less than double the current level of expenditures on these services, and in relative terms, it amounts to just $8.56 per person annually across developing countries (Guttmacher Institute, 2017b). As of 2017, there were 214 million women of reproductive age in developing countries who wanted to control their fertility but did not have access to modern contraceptives. Satisfying this total unmet need for modern contraceptives would prevent 67 million unintended pregnancies, 23 million unplanned births, 36 million induced abortions, and 76,000 maternal deaths each year. If one were to add maternal and newborn healthcare services to the full provision of modern contraceptives, annual maternal mortality would fall even more, from 308,000 to 84,000 maternal deaths, and annual newborn deaths would fall from 2.7 million to 538,000 (Guttmacher Institute, 2017a). It is imperative for US foreign aid policy to support this agenda rather than marginalize women and their reproductive health with ideologically based funding restrictions. Instead of threatening global health funding, US foreign aid policy should support integrated reproductive health services as a cost-effective means of meeting the health needs of vulnerable populations in developing countries.

NOTES

1. These data were not included in the regression analysis because the World Values Survey was not conducted in all 51 countries in the sample during the period of analysis.
2. Professor Catriona Macleod, Rhodes University, South Africa as told to the International Women's Health Coalition.
3. The information and quotations in this paragraph were obtained from an interview I conducted on December 4, 2017, in New York City with an official from IPPF/WHR.
4. See, for example, Angeles, Guilkey, and Mroz (2005), Goldin and Katz (2002), Miller (2010), Aaronson et al. (2017), and Lee and Finlay (2017).
5. Anonymous service provider, Nigeria, as told to Education as a Vaccine (EVA) and the International Women's Health Coalition.
6. This quotation was obtained from an interview I conducted on December 1, 2017, in New York City with Barbara Crane.

APPENDIX

Table A6.1 NUMBER OF INDUCED ABORTIONS AND OBSERVATIONS IN THE DHS SAMPLES BY COUNTRY, 1994–2008

	1994	1995	1996	1997	1998	1999	2000	2001	2002	2003	2004	2005	2006	2007	2008
Latin America and the Caribbean															
Bolivia (BO: 1994, 2003, 2008 DHS)															
Abortions	16	.	.	11	9	16	46	35	46	88	88	97	126	179	37
Obs	6,593	.	.	2,227	4,587	6,539	7,461	8,257	8,432	21,937	15,009	14,344	14,787	15,161	15,111
Brazil (BR: 1996 DHS)															
Abortions	72	87	36	.	.	.	.	.	.	.	.	.	.	.	.
Obs	10,951	11,269	11,278	.	.	.	.	.	.	.	.	.	.	.	.
Colombia (CO: 1995, 2000, 2005, 2010 DHS)															
Abortions	88	86	78	74	112	267	245	221	307	334	462	265	200	241	277
Obs	10,009	19,462	9,713	9,976	10,216	41,008	41,609	31,839	32,404	32,998	72,906	66,340	40,984	41,741	42,368
Dominican Republic (DR: 1996, 1999, 2002 DHS)															
Abortions	55	77	86	39	102	104	156	189	179	.	.	.	.	.	.
Obs	8,349	8,570	8,819	19,698	20,301	20,806	20,186	20,712	21,106	.	.	.	.	.	.

Guatemala (GU: 1995, 1998–99 DHS)

Abortions	29	53	8	8	13	4	·	·	·	·	·	·	·	·	·
Obs	15,736	16,186	5,074	5,280	5,467	4,340	·	·	·	·	·	·	·	·	·

Guyana (GY: 2009 DHS)

Abortions	·	·	·	·	·	·	·	·	·	·	3	14	17	23	43
Obs	·	·	·	·	·	·	·	·	·	·	4,050	4,110	4,191	4,283	4,383

Honduras (HN: 2005–06, 2011–12 DHS)

Abortions	·	·	·	·	·	·	15	30	38	61	65	91	36	59	55
Obs	·	·	·	·	·	·	15,130	15,720	16,237	16,859	17,484	18,142	31,230	17,916	18,600

Nicaragua (NC: 1998, 2001 DHS)

Abortions	39	47	42	63	20	9	10	15	·	·	·	·	·	·	·
Obs	10,984	13,035	14,987	16,829	14,684	5,779	5,900	5,890	·	·	·	·	·	·	·

Peru (PE: 1996, 2000, 2007–08, 2009 DHS)

Abortions	191	297	262	123	146	150	113	55	87	182	247	287	304	312	262
Obs	25,259	48,113	49,290	23,383	24,072	29,839	35,410	15,838	21,420	35,174	54,847	50,390	45,641	40,681	35,470

(continued)

Table A6.1 CONTINUED

	1994	1995	1996	1997	1998	1999	2000	2001	2002	2003	2004	2005	2006	2007	2008
Eastern Europe and Central Asia															
Albania (AL: 2008–09 DHS)															
Abortions	.	.	.	.	.	.	.	.	.	18	22	24	17	16	14
Obs	.	.	.	.	.	.	.	.	.	6,026	6,077	6,126	6,227	6,395	6,480
Armenia (AM: 2000, 2005, 2010 DHS)															
Abortions	.	210	289	312	322	327	303	102	123	148	167	142	66	83	68
Obs	.	5,252	5,334	5,397	5,469	5,539	11,006	5,504	5,501	5,498	5,524	10,568	5,092	5,092	5,047
Azerbaijan (AZ: 2006 DHS)															
Abortions	.	.	.	.	.	.	.	66	154	174	222	250	156	.	.
Obs	.	.	.	.	.	.	.	6,932	7,068	7,221	7,334	7,395	7,330	.	.
Egypt (EG: 1995, 2000, 2005, 2008 DHS)															
Abortions	98	269	50	64	97	74	62	56	81	103	136	139	75	85	59
Obs	13,451	27,672	15,068	14,303	14,018	13,386	31,469	18,305	18,055	33,448	32,676	31,761	14,932	14,438	13,962

Jordan (JO: 1997, 2002, 2007, 2012 DHS)

Abortions	91	84	117	83	50	76	75	83	90	74	99	100	153	118	109
Obs	5,262	5,190	5,090	10,736	5,747	5,677	5,562	5,447	15,869	10,401	10,204	10,005	9,792	20,518	10,891

Kazakhstan (KK: 1999 DHS)

Abortions	86	107	120	124	117	91									
Obs	4,027	4,069	4,128	4,176	4,236	4,218									

Kyrgyz Republic (KY: 2012 DHS)

Abortions	.	.	.	.	.	.	.	.	.	.	.	.	.	18	28
Obs	.	.	.	.	.	.	.	.	.	.	.	.	.	6,586	6,655

Moldova (MB: 2005 DHS)

Abortions	.	.	.	.	.	.	108	120	149	158	166	81	.	.	.
Obs	.	.	.	.	.	.	6,019	6,087	6,168	6,199	6,251	6,186	.	.	.

Morocco (MA: 2003–04 DHS)

Abortions	.	.	.	.	27	43	46	60	64	88	1	.	.	.	.
Obs	.	.	.	.	13,259	13,558	13,947	14,316	14,734	15,001	4,157	.	.	.	.

(*continued*)

Table A6.1 CONTINUED

	1994	1995	1996	1997	1998	1999	2000	2001	2002	2003	2004	2005	2006	2007	2008
Tajikistan (TJ: 2012 DHS)															
Abortions	.	.	.	.	.	.	.	.	.	.	.	.	.	8	19
Obs	.	.	.	.	.	.	.	.	.	.	.	.	.	7,692	7,919
Turkey (TR: 1998, 2003 DHS)															
Abortions	116	107	135	149	184	124	132	140	127	173	21	.	.	.	.
Obs	7,032	7,265	7,517	7,732	15,603	7,771	7,640	7,477	7,306	7,050	4,277	.	.	.	.
Ukraine (UA: 2007 DHS)															
Abortions	.	.	.	.	.	.	.	.	58	77	85	84	65	28	.
Obs	.	.	.	.	.	.	.	.	5,985	5,947	5,901	5,862	5,826	5,703	.
South and Southeast Asia															
Bangladesh (BD: 1996–97, 1999–2000, 2004, 2007, 2011 DHS)															
Abortions	41	95	134	67	89	132	80	64	111	139	90	57	105	136	88
Obs	16,979	17,285	17,539	13,602	19,097	19,370	15,060	10,134	19,807	19,945	20,003	9,901	25,712	25,765	16,186

Cambodia (KH: 2010 DHS)															
Abortions	·	·	·	·	·	·	·	·	·	·	·	16	44	66	94
Obs	·	·	·	·	·	·	·	·	·	·	·	14,829	15,137	15,529	15,951
India (IA: 2005–06 DHS)															
Abortions	·	·	·	·	·	·	38	111	234	286	323	465	184	·	·
Obs	·	·	·	·	·	·	50,843	102,178	105,469	108,647	111,596	113,681	105,830	·	·
Indonesia (ID: 1997, 2002–03, 2007, 2012 DHS)															
Abortions	42	50	46	100	42	49	52	52	110	60	59	53	86	99	65
Obs	27,127	26,639	26,107	53,671	28,159	27,546	26,960	26,346	57,198	41,838	30,732	29,919	29,212	66,597	38,868
Maldives (MV: 2009 DHS)															
Abortions	·	·	·	·	·	·	·	·	·	3	6	14	14	17	33
Obs	·	·	·	·	·	·	·	·	·	6,930	6,984	6,905	6,761	6,590	6,444
Nepal (NP: 2006, 2011 DHS)															
Abortions	·	·	·	·	·	·	6	12	9	24	16	28	39	28	37
Obs	·	·	·	·	·	·	8,174	8,509	8,781	9,109	9,415	19,481	19,882	10,531	10,950

(continued)

Table A6.1 CONTINUED

	1994	1995	1996	1997	1998	1999	2000	2001	2002	2003	2004	2005	2006	2007	2008
Pakistan (PK: 2012–13 DHS)															
Abortions	.	.	.	.	.	.	.	.	.	.	.	.	.	21	35
Obs	.	.	.	.	.	.	.	.	.	.	.	.	.	12,926	12,850
Philippines (PH: 1998, 2003 DHS)															
Abortions	47	56	57	80	36	25	38	45	45	39	.	.	.	.	.
Obs	11,461	11,794	12,228	12,609	23,602	11,196	11,466	11,744	12,068	12,156	.	.	.	.	.
Timor Leste (TL: 2009–10 DHS)															
Abortions	.	.	.	.	.	.	.	.	.	.	0	0	2	2	3
Obs	.	.	.	.	.	.	.	.	.	.	9,861	10,178	10,603	11,052	11,477
Vietnam (VN: 1997, 2002 DHS)															
Abortions	51	74	107	128	109	93	103	111	107	.	.	.	.	.	.
Obs	5,380	5,247	5,151	10,557	5,487	5,334	5,163	5,004	4,817	.	.	.	.	.	.

Sub-Saharan Africa

Benin (BJ: 2006, 2011–12 DHS)

Abortions	.	.	.	.	0	0	0	0	1	3	6	1	4
Obs	.	.	.	.	2,473	6,224	9,213	10,394	11,402	11,450	24,849	13,923	14,285

Burkina Faso (BF: 2003, 2010 DHS)

Abortions	0	0	1	0	2	1	1	1	.	0	4	6	1
Obs	149	1,773	4,421	6,497	7,248	7,842	7,841	7,710	.	13,651	14,022	14,425	14,847

Ethiopia (ET: 2005, 2011 DHS)

Abortions	.	.	.	1	12	15	16	15	19	13	11	9	17
Obs	.	.	.	10,201	10,893	11,319	11,947	12,374	12,739	25,279	12,985	13,563	14,151

Ghana (GH: 2003, 2008 DHS)

Abortions	0	0	0	1	4	3	3	5	6	6	7	23	23
Obs	10	728	1,668	2,412	2,780	3,089	3,113	6,947	4,019	4,167	4,295	4,408	4,469

Guinea (GN: 2005 DHS)

Abortions	.	.	.	0	0	0	1	0	1	0	0	.	.
Obs	.	.	.	682	1,497	3,164	3,929	4,427	4,802	4,799	4,747	.	.

(continued)

Table A6.1 CONTINUED

	1994	1995	1996	1997	1998	1999	2000	2001	2002	2003	2004	2005	2006	2007	2008
Kenya (KE: 1998, 2003, 2008 DHS)															
Abortions	4	12	12	11	10	13	9	16	20	16	5	6	6	21	38
Obs	6,440	6,714	6,943	7,208	13,765	6,805	7,074	7,340	7,550	14,185	6,832	7,073	7,286	7,562	7,738
Madagascar (MD: 2003–04, 2008–09 DHS)															
Abortions	.	.	.	0	0	1	2	2	1	11	19	20	20	36	66
Obs	.	.	.	625	1,862	3,104	3,643	4,148	4,320	17,481	16,510	14,214	14,763	15,342	15,825
Malawi (MW: 2000, 2004, 2010 DHS)															
Abortions	0	1	1	7	4	18	12	9	15	17	48	3	16	15	33
Obs	1,640	4,263	6,454	7,538	8,455	17,791	18,132	10,015	10,310	10,610	10,907	20,703	18,598	19,174	19,814
Mali (ML: 2001, 2006, 2012–13 DHS)															
Abortions	0	0	0	1	1	1	2	4	2	3	0	2	1	1	1
Obs	1,229	3,075	6,125	7,444	8,291	9,187	10,970	14,211	7,742	8,719	9,497	9,570	9,529	8,464	8,731

Mozambique (MZ: 2003, 2011 DHS)															
Abortions	.	.	.	0	1	0	4	6	4	0	0	.	1	5	6
Obs	.	.	.	1,442	3,828	5,871	6,786	7,617	7,773	7,755	73	.	10,735	11,061	11,347
Niger (NI: 2006, 2012 DHS)															
Abortions	.	.	.	.	.	0	0	0	0	1	1	1	0	0	5
Obs	.	.	.	.	.	816	2,123	4,279	5,215	5,808	6,138	6,099	6,050	9,344	9,589
Nigeria (NG: 2008 DHS)															
Abortions	.	.	.	.	.	.	.	.	.	9	17	26	48	45	35
Obs	.	.	.	.	.	.	.	.	.	26,817	27,338	28,307	29,102	29,898	30,382
Rwanda (RW: 2000, 2005, 2010 DHS)															
Abortions	0	1	6	6	6	5	5	3	4	5	10	15	8	5	14
Obs	1,282	3,144	4,455	4,912	6,133	7,052	9,129	4,865	5,346	5,642	5,582	16,094	10,909	11,276	11,575
Senegal (SN: 2005, 2010–11 DHS)															
Abortions	.	.	.	.	0	0	0	3	3	2	2	3	3	6	10
Obs	.	.	.	.	1,056	2,454	5,047	6,398	7,226	7,777	7,770	19,660	12,421	13,129	13,720

(continued)

Table A6.1 CONTINUED

	1994	1995	1996	1997	1998	1999	2000	2001	2002	2003	2004	2005	2006	2007	2008
Sierra Leone (SL: 2008 DHS)															
Abortions	.	.	.	.	.	.	.	.	.	2	2	1	5	10	5
Obs	.	.	.	.	.	.	.	.	.	6,176	6,337	6,586	6,711	6,840	6,824
Swaziland (SZ: 2006–07 DHS)															
Abortions	.	.	.	.	.	.	.	0	0	0	1	3	10	0	.
Obs	.	.	.	.	.	.	.	3,721	3,917	4,086	4,262	4,422	4,580	1,074	.
Tanzania (TZ: 2004–05, 2010 DHS)															
Abortions	.	.	.	.	.	8	12	8	18	27	62	8	9	11	10
Obs	.	.	.	.	.	7,986	8,272	8,621	8,916	9,298	9,524	11,060	8,310	8,611	8,919
Uganda (UG: 2000–01, 2006, 2011 DHS)															
Abortions	0	0	1	3	9	15	8	9	10	13	24	38	22	14	17
Obs	652	2,165	3,547	4,113	4,537	4,668	4,640	9,006	6,851	7,139	7,372	7,670	14,578	6,944	7,228

Zambia (ZM: 2007, 2013–14 DHS)

Abortions	.	.	.	.	.	.	.	.	3	5	9	13	19	11	3
Obs	.	.	.	.	.	.	.	.	5,606	5,826	6,044	6,240	6,506	6,635	12,650

Zimbabwe (ZW: 1994, 1999, 2005–06, 2010–11 DHS)

Abortions	13	11	9	17	20	30	9	17	17	16	28	26	8	7	9
Obs	10,134	4,671	4,889	5,119	5,360	5,507	6,788	7,112	7,451	7,707	8,048	15,391	9,326	7,689	7,916

Note: All samples are constructed using the Individual Recodes of the Demographic and Health Surveys (DHS). Observations are at the level of women per year. The notation "." indicates not available.

Table A6.2 SAMPLE MEANS BY REGION, 1994–2008

	Latin America and the Caribbean				Eastern Europe and Central Asia			
	Mean	SD	Min	Max	Mean	SD	Min	Max
Had induced abortion	0.006	(0.074)	0	1	0.011	(0.106)	0	1
Lives in high-exposure country	0.263	(0.440)	0	1	0.768	(0.422)	0	1
Woman's characteristics								
Age (years)	27.747	(8.384)	15	44	29.231	(8.194)	15	44
Has formal schooling	0.948	(0.222)	0	1	0.772	(0.420)	0	1
Never married	0.251	(0.434)	0	1	0.118	(0.323)	0	1
Lives in urban area	0.694	(0.461)	0	1	0.566	(0.496)	0	1
Country characteristics								
Life expectancy (years)	69.985	(2.972)	57	73	69.600	(2.391)	64	77
Modern contraceptive usage (%)	53.619	(12.442)	18.9	70.5	42.407	(12.793)	14.6	57.6
Abortion law index	2.020	(1.319)	1	7	3.996	(2.664)	1	7

	South and Southeast Asia				Sub-Saharan Africa			
Total non-US aid ($/person)	0.147	(0.293)	0	3.1	0.065	(0.104)	0	0.8
Observations	1,662,006				905,875			
	Mean	SD	Min	Max	Mean	SD	Min	Max
Had induced abortion	0.003	(0.051)	0	1	0.001	(0.032)	0	1
Lives in high-exposure country	0.559	(0.497)	0	1	0.486	(0.500)	0	1
Woman's characteristics								
Age (years)	28.159	(8.168)	15	44	26.624	(7.795)	15	44
Has formal schooling	0.720	(0.449)	0	1	0.588	(0.492)	0	1
Never married	0.096	(0.294)	0	1	0.124	(0.330)	0	1
Lives in urban area	0.343	(0.475)	0	1	0.276	(0.447)	0	1
Country characteristics								
Life expectancy (years)	65.503	(2.239)	61	76	51.979	(5.458)	29	63

(continued)

Table A6.2 CONTINUED

	Latin America and the Caribbean				Eastern Europe and Central Asia			
	Mean	SD	Min	Max	Mean	SD	Min	Max
Modern contraceptive usage (%)	44.988	(9.574)	11.3	56.7	18.427	(13.108)	3.2	59.4
Abortion law index	3.365	(2.597)	0	7	2.587	(1.432)	–	5
Total non-US aid ($/person)	0.179	(0.283)	0	1.4	0.349	(0.581)	0	4.6
Observations	1,876,798				1,839,833			

Note: Observations are at the level of women per year. The total sample has 6,284,512 observations. Standard deviations (SD) in parentheses. Weighted to national levels with DHS sample weights.

Table A6.3 ODDS RATIOS FROM LOGISTIC REGRESSIONS OF INDUCED ABORTION, BY REGION, 1994–2008

	Latin America and the Caribbean			Eastern Europe and Central Asia		
	(1)	(2)	(3)	(1)	(2)	(3)
Policy in effect (2001–08)	0.880	0.922	4.111**	0.879	0.857	0.826
	(0.107)	(0.131)	(2.789)	(0.147)	(0.123)	(0.541)
High exposure	0.663***	0.581***	0.102**	0.498***	0.485***	2.135
	(0.082)	(0.079)	(0.094)	(0.101)	(0.080)	(1.231)
Policy in effect * High exposure	1.595***	1.713***	3.293***	0.549***	0.596***	0.506***
	(0.232)	(0.281)	(0.688)	(0.102)	(0.096)	(0.079)
Woman's age		0.969***	0.968***		0.988**	0.987**
		(0.007)	(0.007)		(0.006)	(0.006)
Woman has formal schooling		1.326**	1.325**		1.265***	1.204***
		(0.174)	(0.175)		(0.093)	(0.072)

(continued)

Table A6.3 CONTINUED

	Latin America and the Caribbean			Eastern Europe and Central Asia		
	(1)	(2)	(3)	(1)	(2)	(3)
Woman never married		0.290***	0.286***		0.034***	0.034***
		(0.046)	(0.044)		(0.020)	(0.020)
Woman lives in urban area		1.524***	1.516***		1.015	1.030
		(0.149)	(0.147)		(0.118)	(0.115)
Country's life expectancy			1.024			0.939
			(0.070)			(0.092)
Country's modern contraceptive usage			0.893**			1.029
			(0.047)			(0.022)
Country's abortion law index			0.916***			1.573*
			(0.028)			(0.430)
Country's total non-US aid			0.538***			1.955**
			(0.083)			(0.557)

	South and Southeast Asia			Sub-Saharan Africa		
	(1)	(2)	(3)	(1)	(2)	(3)
Policy in effect (2001–08)	6.215***	6.895***	6.127***	3.063***	2.895***	4.293**
	(1.752)	(1.837)	(2.049)	(1.059)	(1.032)	(2.803)
High exposure	0.449***	0.513***	1.010	3.832***	2.271***	3.405
	(0.031)	(0.048)	(0.243)	(0.938)	(0.649)	(2.944)
Policy in effect * High exposure	0.279***	0.244***	0.235***	1.891**	1.941**	2.077**
	(0.041)	(0.044)	(0.041)	(0.540)	(0.568)	(0.665)
Intercept	0.007***	0.012***	0.234	0.012***	0.017***	0.013
	(0.001)	(0.004)	(0.993)	(0.001)	(0.003)	(0.097)
Observations	1,662,006	1,662,006	1,662,006	905,875	905,875	905,875

(continued)

Table A6.3 CONTINUED

	South and Southeast Asia			Sub-Saharan Africa		
	(1)	(2)	(3)	(1)	(2)	(3)
Woman's age		0.994	0.994		1.024***	1.024**
		(0.009)	(0.009)		(0.009)	(0.009)
Woman has formal schooling		1.711***	1.705***		2.127***	2.130***
		(0.137)	(0.132)		(0.401)	(0.402)
Woman never married		0.012***	0.012***		0.550***	0.549***
		(0.003)	(0.003)		(0.116)	(0.115)
Woman lives in urban area		1.430***	1.430***		1.478***	1.470***
		(0.082)	(0.082)		(0.092)	(0.094)
Country's life expectancy			1.021			1.000
			(0.092)			(0.034)

Country's modern contraceptive usage			1.003		0.973
			(0.073)		(0.038)
Country's abortion law index			1.083		1.083
			(0.059)		(0.179)
Country's total non-US aid			0.997		0.905
			(0.131)		(0.121)
Intercept	0.009***	0.006***	0.001**	0.000***	0.000***
	(0.001)	(0.002)	(0.002)	(0.000)	(0.000)
Observations	1,876,798	1,876,798	1,876,798	1,839,833	1,839,833

Note: Standard errors, in parentheses, are clustered by country. All regressions include country and year fixed effects. Observations are at the level of women per year. *p < .10. **p < .05. ***p < .01.

Table A7.1 SELF-REPORTED RELIGIOUS DENOMINATIONS AND ATTITUDES TOWARD ABORTION, 2010–2014
(IN PERCENT UNLESS OTHERWISE STATED)

	Muslim	Roman Catholic	Orthodox	Protestant	Hindu/ Buddhist	None	Other	Attitude toward abortion: Never justified	Attitude toward abortion: Mean score (1–10)
Predominantly Muslim									
Tunisia	100	0	0	0	0	0	0	70	2.0
Yemen	100	0	0	0	0	0	0	60	2.4
Palestine	100	0	0	0	0	0	0	56	2.3
Algeria	100	0	0	0	0	0	1	51	2.6
Pakistan	100	0	0	0	0	0	0	77	1.5
Morocco	99	0	0	0	0	0	0	72	1.8
Iraq	99	1	1	0	0	0	0	48	2.5
Turkey	99	0	0	0	0	1	0	66	2.1

Azerbaijan	97	0	2	0	0	1	0	51	2.8
Jordan	97	1	1	0	0	0	0	66	1.9
Libya	96	0	0	0	0	0	4	76	1.8
Uzbekistan	95	0	3	0	0	1	1	51	2.5
Kyrgyzstan	89	0	6	0	0	2	2	55	2.4
Malaysia	63	0	0	0	25	2	11	65	2.1
Lebanon	52	22	11	1	0	0	14	45	3.1
Kazakhstan	50	1	27	1	0	21	0	40	3.5
Nigeria	43	19	2	25	0	9	2	61	2.1
Predominantly Catholic									
Poland	0	92	1	0	0	5	2	44	3.1
Peru	0	73	0	10	0	10	6	57	2.4
Spain	0	72	0	1	0	23	3	18	5.5
Argentina	0	70	0	1	1	17	11	41	3.5

(*continued*)

Table A7.1 CONTINUED

	Muslim	Roman Catholic	Orthodox	Protestant	Hindu/ Buddhist	None	Other	Attitude toward abortion:	
								Never justified	Mean score (1–10)
Mexico	0	70	0	0	0	18	13	62	2.9
Philippines	6	69	0	2	0	10	13	57	3.1
Slovenia	2	65	2	0	0	29	2	12	6.9
Chile	0	64	0	11	0	23	2	43	3.2
Ecuador	0	63	0	0	0	24	14	64	2.1
Colombia	0	61	0	0	0	21	17	73	1.9
Rwanda	5	56	2	20	0	11	6	21	2.2
Brazil	0	53	0	4	0	15	28	70	2.3

Predominantly Orthodox

Georgia	3	1	93	0	0	1	2	68	1.8
Romania	0	3	85	3	0	1	7	55	2.9
Ukraine	1	6	73	2	1	15	3	33	3.8
Belarus	0	11	73	2	0	14	1	31	3.8
Cyprus	25	1	68	0	0	7	1	42	3.6
Russia	7	0	61	1	0	27	4	24	4.4

Predominantly Protestant

Zimbabwe	1	21	1	68	0	8	1	68	2.1
Ghana	11	14	9	58	0	5	3	75	1.6
Trinidad and Tobago	7	20	0	41	21	7	4	64	2.2

Predominantly Hindu or Buddhist

Thailand	2	1	0	0	96	0	1	62	1.9

(continued)

Table A7.1 continued

	Muslim	Roman Catholic	Orthodox	Protestant	Hindu/ Buddhist	None	Other	Attitude toward abortion:	
								Never justified	Mean score (1–10)
India	11	0	0	0	83	0	6	76	1.6
Singapore	16	6	0	10	36	18	14	25	3.8
Predominantly no religion									
China	1	1	0	3	9	81	6	39	2.8
Hong Kong	0	3	0	0	11	69	17	38	3.2
Estonia	0	2	23	8	0	64	3	16	5.0
Netherlands	2	18	0	0	1	64	16	11	6.5
Uruguay	0	24	0	0	0	61	15	42	3.9
Japan	0	0	0	0	37	53	10	12	4.8
Australia	1	23	2	18	2	46	10	16	5.8
South Korea	0	16	0	21	21	41	1	36	3.4

United States	0	22	0	24	1	33	20	22	4.8

Predominantly other religion

Haiti	0	0	0	0	0	0	100	35	3.7
Armenia	0	0	1	0	0	7	93	57	2.3
Sweden	2	1	1	0	0	34	62	5	7.8
South Africa	1	15	0	13	2	16	53	33	4.0
Taiwan	0	1	0	0	27	22	50	28	3.6
New Zealand	1	13	0	13	1	32	40	17	5.2
Germany	6	27	2	0	0	31	35	23	4.5

Source: World Values Survey (2010–2014).

Table A7.2 CORRELATION COEFFICIENTS BETWEEN RELIGION AND
ATTITUDES TOWARD ABORTION

	% who say abortion is never justified	Mean score for abortion is justified (1–10)
% of population that is	Correlation coefficient	Correlation coefficient
Muslim	.45	−.44
Roman Catholic	−.06	.11
Orthodox	−.06	.03
Protestant	.10	−.12
Hindu or Buddhist	.09	−.14
No religion	−.62	.59
Other religion	−.26	.29

Source: Calculated with data from World Values Survey (2010–2014); all data reported in Table A7.1.

Table A7.3 CHANGES IN ATTITUDES TOWARD ABORTION OVER TIME BY PREDOMINANT RELIGION

	% who say abortion is never justified			Mean score for abortion is justified (1–10)		
	1995–1999	2010–2014	Change	1995–1999	2010–2014	Change
Predominantly Muslim						
Azerbaijan	28	51	23	4.4	2.8	–1.6
Nigeria	70	61	–9	2.0	2.1	0.1
Turkey	37	66	30	4.2	2.1	–2.1
Predominantly Roman Catholic						
Argentina	45	41	–4	3.4	3.5	0.1
Brazil	64	70	6	2.5	2.3	–0.2
Chile	68	43	–25	2.2	3.2	1.0
Colombia	74	73	–1	1.9	1.9	0.0
Mexico	57	62	5	2.7	2.9	0.2

(continued)

Table A7.3 CONTINUED

	% who say abortion is never justified			Mean score for abortion is justified (1–10)		
	1995–1999	2010–2014	Change	1995–1999	2010–2014	Change
Peru	62	57	−5	2.3	2.4	0.1
Philippines	58	57	−1	2.3	3.1	0.8
Poland	42	44	2	3.5	3.1	−0.4
Slovenia	25	12	−13	5.7	6.9	1.2
Spain	32	18	−14	4.4	5.5	1.1
Predominantly Orthodox						
Belarus	18	31	12	4.7	3.8	−0.8
Georgia	28	68	40	3.9	1.8	−2.1
Romania	27	55	28	5.0	2.9	−2.0
Russia	16	24	7	4.9	4.4	−0.6
Ukraine	24	33	9	4.3	3.8	−0.5
Predominantly Hindu/Buddhist						
India	52	76	24	2.6	1.6	−0.9

Predominantly no religion

Australia	23	16	-7	4.8	5.8	1.0
China	29	39	10	4.0	2.8	-1.2
Estonia	14	16	2	5.2	5.0	-0.2
Germany	18	23	4	5.5	4.5	-1.0
Japan	21	12	-9	4.4	4.8	0.4
South Korea	37	36	-1	3.4	3.4	0.0
United States	33	22	-10	4.0	4.8	0.9
Uruguay	46	42	-4	3.8	3.9	0.1

Predominantly other religion

Armenia	21	57	36	4.5	2.3	-2.2
New Zealand	17	17	0	5.1	5.2	0.1
South Africa	63	33	-30	2.5	4.0	1.6
Sweden	5	5	0	7.2	7.8	0.6
Taiwan	45	28	-18	2.9	3.6	0.6

Note: Religion classification based on data for 2010–2014. Abortion attitudes for Brazil and Turkey were unavailable for 1995–1999 so were taken from the 1990–1994 survey.

Source: Calculated with data from World Values Survey (2017); all data for 2010–2014 reported in Table A7.1.

REFERENCES

Aaronson, Daniel, Rajeev Dehejia, Andrew Jordan, Cristian Pop-Eleches, Cyrus Samii, and Karl Schulze. 2017. "The Effect of Fertility on Mothers' Labor Supply Over the Last Two Centuries." National Bureau of Economic Research Working Paper No. 23717. Cambridge, MA: NBER.

AbouZahr, Carla. 2003. "Safe Motherhood: A Brief History of the Global Movement 1947–2002." *British Medical Bulletin* 67 (1): 13–25.

ACHPR (African Commission on Human and Peoples' Rights). 2017. *Protocol to the African Charter on Human and Peoples' Rights on the Rights of Women in Africa.* Banjul, Gambia: ACHPR. Available at http://www.achpr.org/instruments/women-protocol/.

ACLU (American Civil Liberties Union). 2006. "ACLU and Public Health Groups Urge Appeals Court to Reject Bush Global AIDS Gag." *ACLU News* (December 21). Available at https://www.aclu.org/news/aclu-and-public-health-groups-urge-appeals-court-reject-bush-global-aids-gag?redirect=cpredirect/27760.

Agarwal, Bina. 2009. "Gender and Forest Conservation: The Impact of Women's Participation in Community Forest Governance." *Ecological Economics* 68 (11): 2785–2799.

Alkema, Leontine, Vladimira Kantorova, Clare Menozzi, and Ann Biddlecom. 2013. "National, Regional, and Global Rates and Trends in Contraceptive Prevalence and Unmet Need for Family Planning between 1990 and 2015: A Systematic and Comprehensive Analysis." *The Lancet* 381 (9878): 1642–1652.

Ananat, Elizabeth, and Daniel Hungerman. 2012. "The Power of the Pill for the Next Generation: Oral Contraception's Effects on Fertility, Abortion, and Maternal and Child Characteristics." *Review of Economics and Statistics* 94 (1): 37–51.

Angeles, Gustavo, David Guilkey, and Thomas Mroz. 2005. "The Effects of Education and Family Planning Programs on Fertility in Indonesia." *Economic Development and Cultural Change* 54 (1): 165–201.

Ashraf, Nava, Erica Field, and Jean Lee. 2014. "Household Bargaining and Excess Fertility: An Experimental Study in Zambia." *American Economic Review* 104 (7): 2210–2237.

Asiedu, Elizabeth, Malokele Nanivazo, and Mwanza Nkusu. 2013. "Determinants of Foreign Aid in Family Planning: How Relevant Is the Mexico City Policy?" WIDER Working Paper 2013/118. Helsinki: UNU-WIDER.

Atighetchi, Dariusch. 2007. *Islamic Bioethics: Problems and Perspectives.* Dordrecht: Springer.

Babiarz, Kimberly, Jiwon Lee, Grant Miller, Tey Nai Peng, and Christine Valente. 2017. "Family Planning and Women's Economic Empowerment: Incentive Effects and Direct Effects Among Malaysian Women." Center for Global Development Working Paper No. 471. Washington, DC: Center for Global Development.

Barot, Sneha, and Susan Cohen. 2015. "The Global Gag Rule and Fights Over Funding UNFPA: The Issues That Won't Go Away." *Guttmacher Policy Review* 18 (2): 27–33.

BBC (British Broadcasting Corporation). 2017. "Chile Abortion: Court Approves Easing Total Ban." *BBC News* (August 21). Available at http://www.bbc.com/news/world-latin-america-41005517.

Becker, Gary. 1960. "An Economic Analysis of Fertility." In Universities-National Bureau (ed.), *Demographic and Economic Change in Developed Countries.* New York: Columbia University Press, pp. 209–240.

———. 1981. *A Treatise on the Family.* Cambridge, MA: Harvard University Press.

Bélanger, Danièle, and Andrea Flynn. 2009. "The Persistence of Induced Abortion in Cuba: Exploring the Notion of an 'Abortion Culture.'" *Studies in Family Planning* 40 (1): 13–26.

Belton, Suzanne, Andrea Whittaker, Zulmira Fonseca, Tanya Wells-Brown, and Patricia Pais. 2009. "Attitudes Towards the Legal Context of Unsafe Abortion in Timor-Leste." *Reproductive Health Matters* 17 (34): 55–64.

Bendavid, Eran, Patrick Avila, and Grant Miller. 2011. "United States Aid Policy and Induced Abortion in Sub-Saharan Africa." *Bulletin of the World Health Organization* 89 (12): 873–880.

Bendavid, Eran, and Jayanta Bhattacharya. 2009. "The President's Emergency Plan for AIDS Relief in Africa: An Evaluation of Outcomes." *Annals of Internal Medicine* 150 (10): 688–695.

Bingenheimer, Jeffrey, and Patty Skuster. 2017. "The Foreseeable Harms of Trump's Global Gag Rule." *Studies in Family Planning* 48 (3): 279–290.

Birdsall, Nancy, Allen Kelley, and Steven Sinding (eds.). 2001. *Population Matters: Demographic Change, Economic Growth, and Poverty in the Developing World.* New York: Oxford University Press.

Blane, John, and Matthew Friedman. 1990. "Mexico City Policy Implementation Study." Population Technical Assistance Project Occasional Paper No. 5. Washington, DC: PTAC.

Bloom, David, David Canning, Günther Fink, and Jocelyn Finlay. 2009. "Fertility, Female Labor Force Participation, and the Demographic Dividend." *Journal of Economic Growth* 14 (2): 79–101.

Boerma, J. Ties, and A. Elisabeth Sommerfelt. 1993. "Demographic and Health Surveys (DHS): Contributions and Limitations." *World Health Statistics Quarterly* 46: 222–226.

Bongaarts, John. 1994. "The Impact of Population Policies: Comment." *Population and Development Review* 20 (3): 616–620.

———. 2014. "The Impact of Family Planning Programs on Unmet Need and Demand for Contraception." *Studies in Family Planning* 45 (2): 247–261.

Bongaarts, John, John Cleland, John Townsend, Jane Bertrand, and Monica Das Gupta. 2012. *Family Planning Programs for the 21st Century: Rationale and Design.* New York: Population Council.

Briggs, Laura. 2002. *Reproducing Empire: Race, Sex, Science, and U.S. Imperialism in Puerto Rico.* Berkeley: University of California Press.

Bryant, John. 2007. "Theories of Fertility Decline and the Evidence From Development Indicators." *Population and Development Review* 33 (1): 101–127.

Bush, George W. 2001. "Reinstatement of the US 'Mexico City Policy.'" *Population and Development Review* 27 (1): 209.

Camp, Sharon. 1987. "The Impact of the Mexico City Policy on Women and Health Care in Developing Countries." *NYU Journal of International Law and Politics* 20: 35–51.

Canning, David, and T. Paul Schultz. 2012. "The Economic Consequences of Reproductive Health and Family Planning." *The Lancet* 380 (9837): 165–171.

Casterline, John, and Steven Sinding. 2000. "Unmet Need for Family Planning in Developing Countries and Implications for Population Policy." *Population and Development Review* 26 (4): 691–723.

Center for American Progress. 2017. "What's at Stake for Women: Threat of the Global Gag Rule." Washington, DC: Center for American Progress. Available at https://www.americanprogress.org/issues/women/reports/2017/01/23/297060/whats-at-stake-for-women-threat-of-the-global-gag-rule/.

Center for Reproductive Rights. 2014. "The World's Abortion Laws Map." New York: Center for Reproductive Rights. Available at https://www.reproductiverights.org/document/the-worlds-abortion-laws-map.

Chen, Lanyan, and Hilary Standing. 2007. "Gender Equity in Transitional China's Healthcare Policy Reforms." *Feminist Economics* 13 (3–4): 189–212.

Cheshes, Jay. 2002. "Hard-Core Philanthropist." *Mother Jones* (November–December). Available at http://www.motherjones.com/politics/2002/09/hard-core-philanthropist-phil-harvey/.

Chowdhury, Elora Halim. 2016. "Development." In Lisa Disch and Mary Hawkesworth (eds.), *The Oxford Handbook of Feminist Theory*. New York: Oxford University Press, pp. 143–163.

Chu, Junhong. 2001. "Prenatal Sex Determination and Sex-Selective Abortion in Rural Central China." *Population and Development Review* 27 (2): 259–281.

Cincotta, Richard, and Barbara Crane. 2001. "The Mexico City Policy and US Family Planning Assistance." *Science* 294 (5542): 525–526.

Cleland, John, Stan Bernstein, Alex Ezeh, Anibal Faundes, Anna Glasier, and Jolene Innis. 2006. "Family Planning: The Unfinished Agenda." *The Lancet* 368 (9549): 1810–1827.

Clinton, William. 1993. "Rescission of the US 'Mexico City Policy.'" *Population and Development Review* 19 (1): 215–216.

Coale, Ansley, and Edgar Hoover. 1958. *Population Growth and Economic Development*. Princeton, NJ: Princeton University Press.

Coelho, Helena Luna, Ana Teixeira, Ana Santos, E. Barros Forte, Silvana Morais, Carlo LaVecchia, Gianni Tognoni, and Andrew Herxheimer. 1993. "Misoprostol and Illegal Abortion in Fortaleza, Brazil." *The Lancet* 341 (8855): 1261–1263.

Crane, Barbara. 1994. "The Transnational Politics of Abortion." *Population and Development Review* 20 (Supplement): 241–262.

Crane, Barbara, Nils Daulaire, and Alex Ezeh. 2017. "Reproductive Health in Culture Wars Crossfire." *Science* 358 (6360): 175–176.

Crane, Barbara, and Jennifer Dusenberry. 2004. "Power and Politics in International Funding for Reproductive Health: The US Global Gag Rule." *Reproductive Health Matters* 12 (24): 128–137.

Crossette, Barbara. 2005. "Reproductive Health and the Millennium Development Goals: The Missing Link." *Studies in Family Planning* 36 (1): 71–79.

Daniels, Cynthia, Janna Ferguson, Grace Howard, and Amanda Roberti. 2016. "Informed or Misinformed Consent? Abortion Policy in the United States." *Journal of Health Politics, Policy and Law* 41 (2): 181–209.

Davies, Christian. 2016. "Poland's Abortion Ban Proposal Near Collapse After Mass Protests." *The Guardian* (October 5). Available at https://www.theguardian.com/world/2016/oct/05/polish-government-performs-u-turn-on-total-abortion-ban.

Debpuur, Cornelius, James Phillips, Elizabeth Jackson, Alex Nazzar, Pierre Ngom, and Fred Binka. 2002. "The Impact of the Navrongo Project on Contraceptive Knowledge and Use, Reproductive Preferences, and Fertility." *Studies in Family Planning* 33 (2): 141–164.

Devereux, George. 1976. *A Study of Abortion in Primitive Societies: A Typological, Distributional, and Dynamic Analysis of the Prevention of Birth in 400 Preindustrial Societies*. New York: International Universities Press.

Dixon-Mueller, Ruth. 1993. *Population Policy & Women's Rights: Transforming Reproductive Choice*. Westport, CT: Praeger Publishers.

DKT International. 2017. *DKT International Annual Report 2017*. Washington, DC: DKT International. Available at https://www.dktinternational.org/resources/annual-reports/.

Doan, Alesha. 2007. *Opposition and Intimidation: The Abortion Wars and Strategies of Political Harassment*. Ann Arbor: University of Michigan Press.

Durrance, Christine. 2013. "The Effects of Increased Access to Emergency Contraception on Sexually Transmitted Disease and Abortion Rates." *Economic Inquiry* 51 (3): 1682–1695.

Easterlin, Richard. 1975. "An Economic Framework for Fertility Analysis." *Studies in Family Planning* 6 (3): 54–63.

———. 1978. "The Economics and Sociology of Fertility: A Synthesis." In Charles Tilly (ed.), *Historical Studies of Changing Fertility*. Princeton, NJ: Princeton University Press, pp. 57–113.

Easterly, William. 2006. *The White Man's Burden: Why the West's Efforts to Aid the Rest Have Done So Much Ill and So Little Good*. New York: Penguin.

Easterly, William, and Claudia Williamson. 2011. "Rhetoric versus Reality: The Best and Worst of Aid Agency Practices." *World Development* 39 (11): 1930–1949.

Economist. 2016. "How to Make Abortion Rarer." *The Economist* (December 3). Available at https://www.economist.com/news/international/21711025-bans-and-restrictions-do-not-work-superior-birth-control-does-how-make-abortion-rarer.

Ehrlich, Paul. 1968. *The Population Bomb*. New York: Sierra Club / Ballantine Books.

Elson, Diane, and Nilüfer Çağatay. 2000. "The Social Content of Macroeconomic Policies." *World Development* 28 (7): 1347–1364.

Elul, Batya, Selma Hajri, Charlotte Ellertson, Claude Ben Slama, Elizabeth Pearlman, and Beverly Winikoff. 2001. "Can Women in Less-Developed Countries Use a Simplified Medical Abortion Regimen?" *The Lancet* 357 (9266): 1402–1405.

Erdman, Joanna. 2011. "Access to Information on Safe Abortion: A Harm Reduction and Human Rights Approach." *Harvard Journal of Law and Gender* 34 (2): 413–462.

Faúndes, Anibal, and Iqbal Shah. 2015. "Evidence Supporting Broader Access to Safe Legal Abortion." *International Journal of Gynecology & Obstetrics* 131 (S1): S56–S59.

Fetters, Tamara, and Ghazaleh Samandari. 2015. "Abortion Incidence in Cambodia, 2005 and 2010." *Global Public Health* 10 (4): 532–544.

Filopovic, Jill. 2017. "The Global Gag Rule: America's Deadly Export." *Foreign Policy* (March 20). Available at http://foreignpolicy.com/2017/03/20/.

Finkle, Jason, and Barbara Crane. 1985. "Ideology and Politics at Mexico City: The United States at the 1984 International Conference on Population." *Population and Development Review* (1985): 1–28.

Folbre, Nancy. 1983. "Of Patriarchy Born: The Political Economy of Fertility Decisions." *Feminist Studies* 9 (2): 261–284.

FP2020 (Family Planning 2020) Partnership. 2017. *FP2020: The Way Ahead 2016–2017.* Available at http://progress.familyplanning2020.org/en/resources.

Frejka, Tomas. 1983. "Induced Abortion and Fertility: A Quarter Century of Experience in Eastern Europe." *Population and Development Review* 9 (3): 494–520.

Gerdts, Caitlin, Divya Vohra, and Jennifer Ahern. 2013. "Measuring Unsafe Abortion-Related Mortality: A Systematic Review of the Existing Methods." *PLOS ONE* 8 (1): e53346.

Gertler, Paul, and Jack Molyneaux. 1994. "How Economic Development and Family Planning Programs Combined to Reduce Indonesian Fertility." *Demography* 31 (1): 33–63.

Gezinski, Lindsay. 2012. "The Global Gag Rule: Impacts of Conservative Ideology on Women's Health." *International Social Work* 55 (6): 837–849.

Gladstone, Rick. 2017. "A Woman's Voice for Women at the U.N. Agency for Reproductive Rights." *New York Times* (December 15). Available at https://www.nytimes.com/2017/12/15/world/americas/natalia-kanem-profile-unfpa.html.

Glasier, Anna, Karen Fairhurst, Sally Wyke, Sue Ziebland, Peter Seaman, Jeremy Walker, and Fatim Lakha. 2004. "Advanced Provision of Emergency Contraception Does Not Reduce Abortion Rates." *Contraception* 69 (5): 361–366.

Glasier, Anna, A. Metin Gülmezoglu, George Schmid, Claudia Garcia Moreno, and Paul Van Look. 2006. "Sexual and Reproductive Health: A Matter of Life and Death." *The Lancet* 368 (9547): 1595–1607.

Goldberg, Michelle. 2009. *The Means of Reproduction: Sex, Power, and the Future of the World.* New York: Penguin.

Goldin, Claudia, and Lawrence Katz. 2002. "The Power of the Pill: Oral Contraceptives and Women's Career and Marriage Decisions." *Journal of Political Economy* 110 (4): 730–770.

Gomperts, R., K. Jelinska, S. Davies, K. Gemzell-Danielsson, and G. Kleiverda. 2008. "Using Telemedicine for Termination of Pregnancy with Mifepristone and Misoprostol in Settings Where There Is No Access to Safe Services." *BJOG: An International Journal of Obstetrics & Gynaecology* 115 (9): 1171–1178.

González Vélez, Ana Cristina. 2012. "'The Health Exception': A Means of Expanding Access to Legal Abortion." *Reproductive Health Matters* 20 (40): 22–29.

Goodkind, Daniel. 1996. "On Substituting Sex Preference Strategies in East Asia: Does Prenatal Sex Selection Reduce Postnatal Discrimination?" *Population and Development Review* 22 (1): 111–125.

Gramer, Robbie. 2017. "Proposed U.S. Cuts to AIDS Funding Could Cause Millions of Deaths: Report." *Foreign Policy* (December 1). Available at http://foreignpolicy.com/2017/12/01/proposed-u-s-cuts-to-aids-funding-could-cause-millions-of-deaths-report-world-aids-day-hiv-global-health-pepfar-state-department-trump-one-campaign/.

Greenhalgh, Susan (ed.). 1995. *Situating Fertility: Anthropology and Demographic Inquiry.* Cambridge: Cambridge University Press.

———. 1996. "The Social Construction of Population Science: An Intellectual, Institutional, and Political History of Twentieth-Century Demography." *Comparative Studies in Society and History* 38 (1): 26–66.

Grimes, David, Janie Benson, Susheela Singh, Mariana Romero, Bela Ganatra, Friday Okonofua, and Iqbal Shah. 2006. "Unsafe Abortion: The Preventable Pandemic." *The Lancet* 368 (9550): 1908–1919.

Grossu, Arina. 2017. "I'm Grateful for the Restoration of the Mexico City Policy This International Women's Day." Available at http://www.frc.org/op-eds/ im-grateful-for-the-restoration-of-the-mexico-city-policy-this-international- womens-day.

Guinnane, Timothy. 2011. "The Historical Fertility Transition: A Guide for Economists." *Journal of Economic Literature* 49 (3): 589–614.

Guttmacher Institute 2017a. *Our Work by Geography: Country Fact Sheets.* New York: Guttmacher Institute. Available at https://www.guttmacher.org/ geography.

———. 2017b. *Adding It Up: Investing in Contraception and Maternal and Newborn Health, 2017.* New York: Guttmacher Institute. Available at https://www. guttmacher.org/fact-sheet/adding-it-up-contraception-mnh-2017.

Hanmer, Lucia, and Jeni Klugman. 2016. "Exploring Women's Agency and Empowerment in Developing Countries: Where Do We Stand." *Feminist Economics* 22 (1): 237–263.

Heaton, Laura, Paul Bouey, Joe Fu, John Stover, Timothy Fowler, Rob Lyerla, and Mary Mahy. 2015. "Estimating the Impact of the US President's Emergency Plan for AIDS Relief on HIV Treatment and Prevention Programmes in Africa." *Sexually Transmitted Infections* 91 (8): 615–620.

Hodgson, Dennis, and Susan Cotts Watkins. 1997. "Feminists and Neo-Malthusians: Past and Present Alliances." *Population and Development Review* 23(3): 469–523.

HRW (Human Rights Watch). 2017. "Re: Early Impact of the Protecting Life in Global Health Assistance Policy in Kenya and Uganda." New York: Human Rights Watch. Available at https://www.hrw.org/news/2017/10/26/re-early- impact-protecting-life-global-health-assistance-policy-kenya-and-uganda.

ICEC (International Consortium for Emergency Contraception). 2017. *EC Pill Types and Countries of Availability, By Brand.* New York: ICEC. Available at http://www.cecinfo.org/country-by-country-information/status-availability- database/ec-pill-types-and-countries-of-availability-by-brand/.

IHME (Institute for Health Metrics and Evaluation). 2017. *Financing Global Health 2016: Development Assistance, Public and Private Health Spending for the Pursuit of Universal Health Coverage.* Seattle, WA: IHME. Available at http://www. healthdata.org/policy-report/financing-global-health-2016-development- assistance-public-and-private-health-spending.

IPPF (International Planned Parenthood Federation). 2015. *Annual Performance Report 2015*. London: IPPF. Available at http://www.ippf.org/sites/default/files/2016-06/annualperformancereport2015.pdf.

Jaffré, Yannick, and Siri Suh. 2016. "Where the Lay and the Technical Meet: Using an Anthropology of Interfaces to Explain Persistent Reproductive Health Disparities in West Africa." *Social Science & Medicine* 156: 175–183.

Johnson, Lyndon B. 1965. "Annual Message to the Congress on the State of the Union." Santa Barbara, CA: The American Presidency Project. Available at http://www.presidency.ucsb.edu/ws/?pid=26907.

Jones, Kelly. 2015. "Contraceptive Supply and Fertility Outcomes: Evidence from Ghana." *Economic Development and Cultural Change* 64 (1): 31–69.

Jones, Rachel, and Jenna Jerman. 2017. "Population Group Abortion Rates and Lifetime Incidence of Abortion: United States, 2008–2014." *American Journal of Public Health* (October 19): e1–e6.

Joshi, Shareen, and T. Paul Schultz. 2013. "Family Planning and Women's and Children's Health: Long-term Consequences of an Outreach Program in Matlab, Bangladesh." *Demography* 50 (1): 149–180.

Kabeer, Naila, Lopita Huq, and Simeen Mahmud. 2014. "Diverging Stories of "Missing Women." In South Asia: Is Son Preference Weakening in Bangladesh?" *Feminist Economics* 20 (4): 138–163.

Kaiser Family Foundation. 2017a. *The Mexico City Policy: An Explainer*. Henry J. Kaiser Family Foundation. Available at http://www.kff.org/global-health-policy/fact-sheet/mexico-city-policy-explainer/.

———. 2017b. *The U.S. Government Engagement in Global Health: A Primer*. Henry J. Kaiser Family Foundation. Available at http://files.kff.org/attachment/report-the-u-s-government-engagement-in-global-health-a-primer.

Kasinof, Laura. 2017. "Trump's 'Global Gag Rule on Steroids' Threatens Congolese Clinics." *Public Radio International* (November 3). Available at https://www.pri.org/stories/2017-11-03/trumps-global-gag-rule-steriods-threatens-congolese-clinics.

Kassebaum, Nicholas, et al. 2014. "Global, Regional, and National Levels and Causes of Maternal Mortality During 1990–2013: A Systematic Analysis for the Global Burden of Disease Study 2013." *The Lancet* 384 (9947): 980–1004.

Kates, Jennifer, and Kellie Moss. 2017. *What Is the Scope of the Mexico City Policy: Assessing Abortion Laws in Countries That Receive U.S. Global Health Assistance*. Henry J. Kaiser Family Foundation. Available at https://www.kff.org/global-health-policy/issue-brief/what-is-the-scope-of-the-mexico-city-policy-assessing-abortion-laws-in-countries-that-receive-u-s-global-health-assistance/.

Khan, Khalid, Daniel Wojdyla, Lale Say, A. Metin Gülmezoglu, and Paul Van Look. 2006. "WHO Analysis of Causes of Maternal Death: A Systematic Review." *The Lancet* 367 (9516): 1066–1074.

Kulczycki, Andrzej. 1999. *The Abortion Debate in the World Arena*. New York: Routledge.

————. 2007. "Ethics, Ideology, and Reproductive Health Policy in the United States." *Studies in Family Planning* 38 (4): 333–351.

Kumar, Anuradha, Leila Hessini, and Ellen Mitchell. 2009. "Conceptualising Abortion Stigma." *Culture, Health & Sexuality* 11 (6): 625–639.

Labandera, Ana, Monica Gorgoroso, and Leonel Briozzo. 2016. "Implementation of the Risk and Harm Reduction Strategy against Unsafe Abortion in Uruguay: From a University Hospital to the Entire Country." *International Journal of Gynecology & Obstetrics* 134 (S1): S7–S11.

Lam, David. 2011. "How the World Survived the Population Bomb: Lessons from 50 Years of Extraordinary Demographic History." *Demography* 48 (4): 1231–1262.

Lee, Marlene, and Jocelyn Finlay. 2017. *The Effect of Reproductive Health Improvements on Women's Economic Empowerment*. Washington, DC: Population and Poverty Research Network. Available at http://www.prb.org/pdf17/17-246_POPPOV_Women_Empower.pdf.

Levine, Phillip. 2004. *Sex and Consequences: Abortion, Public Policy, and the Economics of Fertility*. Princeton, NJ: Princeton University Press.

Lief, Eric, Adam Wexler, and Jen Kates. 2017. *Donor Government Funding for Family Planning in 2016*. Henry J. Kaiser Family Foundation. Available at http://files.kff.org/attachment/Report-Donor-Government-Funding-for-Family-Planning-in-2016.

Long, J. Scott, and Jeremy Freese. 2014. *Regression Models for Categorical Dependent Variables Using Stata, Third Edition*. College Station, TX: Stata Press.

Magnani, Robert, Naomi Rutenberg, and H. Gilman McCann. 1996. "Detecting Induced Abortions from Reports of Pregnancy Terminations in DHS Calendar Data." *Studies in Family Planning* 27 (1): 36–43.

Marston, Cicely, and John Cleland. 2003. "Relationships Between Contraception and Abortion: A Review of the Evidence." *International Family Planning Perspectives* 29 (1): 6–13.

McCann, Carole. 2016. *Figuring the Population Bomb: Gender and Demography in the Mid-Twentieth Century*. Seattle: University of Washington Press.

McKelvey, Christopher, Duncan Thomas, and Elizabeth Frankenberg. 2012. "Fertility Regulation in an Economic Crisis." *Economic Development and Cultural Change* 61 (1): 7–38.

Miller, Grant. 2010. "Contraception as Development? New Evidence from Family Planning in Colombia." *The Economic Journal* 120 (545): 709–736.

Miller, Grant, and Kimberly Babiarz. 2016. "Family Planning Program Effects: Evidence from Microdata." *Population and Development Review* 42 (1): 7–26.

Miller, Grant, and Christine Valente. 2016. "Population Policy: Abortion and Modern Contraception are Substitutes." *Demography* 53 (4): 979–1009.

Molyneaux, John, and Paul Gertler. 2000. "The Impact of Targeted Family Planning Programs in Indonesia." *Population and Development Review* 26 (supplement): 61–85.

Morgan, Lynn, and Elizabeth Roberts. 2012. "Reproductive Governance in Latin America." *Anthropology & Medicine* 19 (2): 241–254.

Moss, Kellie, and Jennifer Kates. 2017. *How Many Foreign NGOs Are Subject to the Expanded Mexico City Policy?* Henry J. Kaiser Family Foundation. Available at http://files.kff.org/attachment/Issue-Brief-How-Many-Foreign-NGOs-Are-Subject-to-the-Expanded-Mexico-City-Policy.

Moyo, Dambisa. 2009. *Dead Aid: Why Aid Is Not Working and How There Is a Better Way for Africa.* New York: Farrar, Straus, and Giroux.

MSI (Marie Stopes International). 2015a. *Financial Statements and Annual Report 2015.* London: MSI. Available at https://www.mariestopes.org/media/2144/financial-statements-2015.pdf.

———. 2015b. *Global Impact Report 2015: Scaling Up Excellence.* London: MSI. Available at https://mariestopes.org/media/2137/global-impact-report-2015.pdf.

———. 2017. "The Mexico City Policy: A World Without Choice." London: MSI. Available at https://mariestopes.org/what-we-do/our-approach/policy-and-advocacy/the-mexico-city-policy-a-world-without-choice/.

Murphy, Michelle. 2012. *Seizing the Means of Reproduction: Entanglements of Feminism, Health, and Technoscience.* Durham, NC: Duke University Press.

Ngwena, Charles. 2010. "Inscribing Abortion as a Human Right: Significance of the Protocol on the Rights of Women in Africa." *Human Rights Quarterly* 32 (4): 783–864.

Nixon, Richard. 1969. "Special Message to the Congress on Problems of Population Growth." Santa Barbara, CA: The American Presidency Project. Available at http://www.presidency.ucsb.edu/ws/?pid=2132.

Noble, Jeanne, and Malcolm Potts. 1996. "The Fertility Transition in Cuba and the Federal Republic of Korea: The Impact of Organised Family Planning." *Journal of Biosocial Science* 28 (2): 211–225.

Notestein, Frank. 1945. "Population: The Long View." In Theodore Schultz (ed.), *Food for the World.* Chicago: University of Chicago Press, pp. 36–57.

———. 1953. "Economic Problems of Population Change." In *Proceedings of the Eighth International Conference of Agricultural Economists.* London: Oxford University Press, pp. 13–31.

NRLC (National Right to Life Committee). 2017. "Trump Restores Policy Preventing Organizations That Promote Abortion Overseas From Receiving U.S. Foreign Aid." Available at http://www.nrlc.org/communications/releases/2017/release012317/.

Obama, Barack. 2009. "Revocation of the Reinstatement of the 'Mexico City Policy' on US Family Planning Assistance." *Population and Development Review* 35 (1): 215–216.

OECD (Organization for Economic Cooperation and Development). 2017. *Creditor Reporting System Database.* Available at https://stats.oecd.org/Index.aspx?DataSetCode=CRS1.

Okeowo, Alexis. 2011. "Africa's Abortion Wars." *New York Times* (December 15). Available at https://latitude.blogs.nytimes.com/2011/12/15/africas-abortion-wars/.

PAI (Population Action International). 2015. *A Reproductive Health Index: Rights and Results.* Washington, DC: PAI. Available at https://pai.org/wp-content/uploads/2015/05/RHIreport.pdf.

———. 2005. *Access Denied: U.S. Restrictions on International Family Planning.* Washington, DC: PAI. Available at https://pai.org/ggrresources/.

Panda, Pradeep, and Bina Agarwal. 2005. "Marital Violence, Human Development and Women's Property Status in India." *World Development* 33 (5): 823–850.

PBS (Public Broadcasting Service). 2017. "Impact of 'Global Gag Rule' Goes Beyond Abortion for these Health Groups in Kenya." *PBS News Hour* (December 19). Available at https://www.pbs.org/newshour/show/impact-of-global-gag-rule-goes-beyond-abortion-for-these-health-groups-in-kenya.

PEPFAR (President's Emergency Plan for AIDS Relief). 2017. "PEPFAR Fact Sheet: 2017 PEPFAR Latest Global Results." Available at https://www.pepfar.gov/documents/organization/276321.pdf.

Petchesky, Rosalind. 1990. *Abortion and Woman's Choice: The State, Sexuality and Reproductive Freedom.* Boston, MA: Northeastern University Press.

Polis, Chelsea, Sarah Bradley, Akinrinola Bankole, Tsuyoshi Onda, Trevor Croft, and Susheela Singh. 2016. *Contraceptive Failure Rates in the Developing World: An Analysis of Demographic and Health Survey Data in 43 Countries.* New York: Guttmacher Institute. Available at https://www.guttmacher.org/report/contraceptive-failure-rates-in-developing-world.

Pop-Eleches, Cristian. 2006. "The Impact of an Abortion Ban on Socioeconomic Outcomes of Children: Evidence from Romania." *Journal of Political Economy* 114 (4): 744–773.

Pritchett, Lant. 1994. "Desired Fertility and the Impact of Population Policies." *Population and Development Review* 20 (1): 1–55.

Rahman, Mizanur, Julie DaVanzo, and Abdur Razzaque. 2001. "Do Better Family Planning Services Reduce Abortion in Bangladesh?" *The Lancet* 358 (9287): 1051–1056.

Randall, Amy. 2011. "'Abortion Will Deprive You of Happiness!' Soviet Reproductive Politics in the Post-Stalin Era." *Journal of Women's History* 23 (3): 13–38.

Robinson, Rachel. 2010. "UNFPA in Context: An Institutional History." Center for Global Development Background Paper. Washington, DC: Center for Global Development. Available at https://www.cgdev.org/doc/UNFPA-in-Context.pdf.

Rosenfield, Allan, and Deborah Maine. 1985. "Maternal Mortality - A Neglected Tragedy: Where Is the M in MCH?" *The Lancet* 326 (8446): 83–85.

Ross, John, Eva Weissman, and John Stover. 2009. "Contraceptive Projections and the Donor Gap." Reproductive Health Supplies Coalition. Brussels: RHSC.

Available at https://www.rhsupplies.org/uploads/tx_rhscpublications/RHSC-FundingGap-Final.pdf.

Say, Lale, Doris Chou, Alison Gemmill, Özge Tunçalp, Ann-Beth Moller, Jane Daniels, A. Metin Gülmezoglu, Marleen Temmerman, and Leontine Alkema. 2014. "Global Causes of Maternal Death: A WHO Systematic Analysis." *The Lancet Global Health* 2 (6): e323–e333.

Sedgh, Gilda, Jonathan Bearak, Susheela Singh, Akinrinola Bankole, Anna Popinchalk, Bela Ganatra, Clémentine Rossier et al. 2016. "Abortion Incidence Between 1990 and 2014: Global, Regional, and Subregional Levels and Trends." *The Lancet* 388 (10041): 258–267.

Sen, Amartya. 1989. "Women's Survival as a Development Problem." *Bulletin of American Academy of Arts and Sciences* 18 (2): 14–29.

Sinding, Steven. 2007. "Overview and Perspective." In Warren Robinson and John Ross (eds.), *The Global Family Planning Revolution: Three Decades of Population Policies and Programs*. Washington, DC: World Bank, pp. 1–12.

Singh, Jerome, and Salim Karim. 2017. "Trump's 'Global Gag Rule': Implications for Human Rights and Global Health." *The Lancet Global Health* 5 (4): e387–e389.

Singh, Susheela, and Isaac Maddow-Zimet. 2016. "Facility-Based Treatment for Medical Complications Resulting from Unsafe Pregnancy Termination in the Developing World, 2012: A Review of Evidence from 26 Countries." *BJOG: An International Journal of Obstetrics & Gynaecology* 123 (9): 1489–1498.

Sinha, Nistha. 2005. "Fertility, Child Work, and Schooling Consequences of Family Planning Programs: Evidence From an Experiment in Rural Bangladesh." *Economic Development and Cultural Change* 54 (1): 97–128.

Smyth, Ines. 1996. "Gender Analysis of Family Planning: Beyond the Feminist vs. Population Control Debate." *Feminist Economics* 2 (2): 63–86.

Sneeringer, Robyn, Deborah Billings, Bela Ganatra, and Traci Baird. 2012. "Roles of Pharmacists in Expanding Access to Safe and Effective Medical Abortion in Developing Countries: A Review of the Literature." *Journal of Public Health Policy* 33 (2): 218–229.

Starrs, Ann. 2017. "The Trump Global Gag Rule: An Attack on US Family Planning and Global Health Aid." *The Lancet* 389 (10068): 485–486.

Storeng, Katerini, and Dominique Béhague. 2014. "'Playing the Numbers Game': Evidence-Based Advocacy and the Technocratic Narrowing of the Safe Motherhood Initiative." *Medical Anthropology Quarterly* 28 (2): 260–279.

Suh, Siri. 2015. "'Right Tool,' Wrong 'Job': Manual Vacuum Aspiration, Post-Abortion Care and Transnational Population Politics in Senegal." *Social Science & Medicine* 135: 56–66.

———. 2017. "Accounting for Abortion: Accomplishing Transnational Reproductive Governance Through Post-Abortion Care in Senegal." *Global Public Health* (DOI 10.1080/17441692.2017.1301513): 1–18.

Swetlitz, Ike. 2017. "Foreign Health Groups Cutting Services After a White House Decision on Abortion Funding." *STAT* (November 8). Available at https://www.statnews.com/2017/11/08/abortion-usaid-womens-health/.

Swidler, Ann, and Susan Cotts Watkins. 2009. "'Teach a Man to Fish': The Sustainability Doctrine and Its Social Consequences." *World Development* 37 (7): 1182–1196.

Taylor, Jamila, and Anu Kumar. 2011. "How Existing US Policy Limits Global Health and the Achievement of Millennium Development Goals to Improve Maternal Health and Promote Gender Equality." *Yale Journal of International Affairs* 6: 43–52.

Trump, Donald. 2017. "Restoration of the US 'Mexico City Policy' by President Donald J. Trump." *Population and Development Review* 43 (1): 188.

UCLA Institute for Digital Research and Education. 2017. "Deciphering Interactions in Logistic Regression." Available at https://stats.idre.ucla.edu/stata/seminars/deciphering-interactions-in-logistic-regression/.

UNDESA (United Nations, Department of Economic and Social Affairs), Population Division. 2014. *Abortion Policies and Reproductive Health around the World.* New York: UNDESA. Available at http://www.un.org/en/development/desa/population/publications/pdf/policy/AbortionPoliciesReproductiveHealth.pdf.

———. 2015a. *World Fertility Data 2015.* New York: UNDESA. Available at http://www.un.org/en/development/desa/population/publications/dataset/fertility/wfd2015.shtml.

———. 2015b. World Population Policies Database. New York: UNDESA. Available at https://esa.un.org/poppolicy/about_database.aspx.

———. 2017. *Model-Based Estimates and Projections of Family Planning Indicators 2017.* New York: UNDESA. Available at http://www.un.org/en/development/desa/population/theme/family-planning/cp_model.shtml.

UNFPA (United Nations Population Fund). 2017. *Financial Resource Flows for Population Activities.* New York: UNFPA. Available at http://www.unfpa.org/publications.

USAID (United States Agency for International Development). 2017. "Family Planning Timeline." Washington, DC: USAID. Available at https://www.usaid.gov/sites/default/files/documents/1864/timeline_b.pdf.

USCCB (United States Conference of Catholic Bishops). 2017 "USCCB Pro Life Chairman Applauds Reestablishment of Mexico City Policy." Available at http://www.usccb.org/news/2017/17-018.cfm.

van Dalen, Hendrik, and Maja Scharf. 2013. "Reproductive Health Aid: A Delicate Balancing Act." In Andrzej Kulczycki (ed.), *Critical Issues in Reproductive Health.* New York: Springer, pp. 195–214.

Vlassoff, Michael, Susheela Singh, and Tsuyoshi Onda. 2016. "The Cost of Post-Abortion Care in Developing Countries: A Comparative Analysis of Four Studies." *Health Policy and Planning* 31 (8): 1020–1030.

Westoff, Charles. 2008. "A New Approach to Estimating Abortion Rates." DHS Analytical Studies No. 13. Calverton, MD: Macro International. Available at https://dhsprogram.com/pubs/pdf/AS13/AS13.pdf.

Westoff, Charles, Almaz Sharmanov, Jeremiah Sullivan, and Trevor Croft. 1998. *Replacement of Abortion by Contraception in Three Central Asian Republics.* Calverton, MD: Policy Project and Macro International. Available at http://citeseerx.ist.psu.edu/viewdoc/download?doi=10.1.1.579.2012&rep=rep1&type=pdf

White House Office of Policy Development. 1984. "US Policy Statement for the International Conference on Population." *Population and Development Review* 10 (3): 574–579.

Winikoff, Beverly, Irving Sivin, Kurus Coyaji, Evelio Cabezas, Xiao Bilian, Gu Sujuan, Du Ming-kun, Usha Krishna, Andrea Eschen, and Charlotte Ellertson. 1997. "Safety, Efficacy, and Acceptability of Medical Abortion in China, Cuba, and India: A Comparative Trial of Mifepristone-Misoprostol Versus Surgical Abortion." *American Journal of Obstetrics and Gynecology* 176 (2): 431–437.

WHO (World Health Organization). 2011. *Unsafe Abortion: Global and Regional Estimates of the Incidence of Unsafe Abortion and Associated Mortality in 2008.* Geneva: WHO. Available at http://www.who.int/reproductivehealth/publications/unsafe_abortion/9789241501118/en/

———. 2015. *The Global Strategy for Women's, Children's and Adolescents' Health (2016–2030).* Geneva: WHO. Available at http://www.who.int/life-course/partners/global-strategy/en/.

World Bank. 2017. World Development Indicators Database. Available at http://databank.worldbank.org/data/reports.aspx?source=world-development-indicators.

World Values Survey. 2017. *World Value Survey 1981–2014 Longitudinal Aggregate v.20150418.* Madrid: JD Systems (Aggregate File Producer). Available at http://www.worldvaluessurvey.org.

Worldwatch Institute. 2016. *Family Planning and Environmental Sustainability: Assessing the Science.* Washington, DC: Worldwatch Institute. Available at http://fpesa.net/wp-content/uploads/2016/06/16-118_WW_FPESAReport-working-links.pdf.

INDEX